Sapience Publishing. First Edition, 2024.

www.sapienceinstitute.org

CONTENTS

INTRODUCTION
A STORY TO TELL

We all love stories; we love to hear them; we love to tell them. Humans have long used storytelling to relay their most intimate of emotions. Whether fact or fiction, stories have afforded humanity a chance to both express and search within themselves. Often the storyteller is as captivated by the story as the listener— for stories capture something of the human condition that is irresistible.

Storytelling is unique to humans, and as a sociocultural phenomenon, storytelling is the thread which binds humanity's history with its present. Storytelling is what has brought us this far, each narrator building upon the understanding of the one who preceded him.

All of us have a story to tell. Our lives are tapestries with memories, loves, hates, pleasures, and agonies. Parts of this tapestry are jewel-encrusted, and other parts are torn and tattered. No two stories are identical, and no one's story is meaningless. Regardless of where life has taken us and in what contexts we have found ourselves, all stories have universal truths and life-affirming maxims that one can learn from.

We all share the human condition, along with the inescapable familiarity this affords us. However much we wish to differentiate ourselves, our substance and the problems we face remain identical. Two men may be enemies, but through a story—fact or fiction—they both relate to, they are able to find common ground and common truths.

Each human who passes through the stages of life will face the same existential questions: "What am I?", "Why am I here?", "Where am I headed?", "What is my purpose?" This book is my story. It is a recollection of my life and how I dealt with these unsettling questions, and through it, I am sure you will find something that you can connect with, something that all people can connect with. And I hope that these points of connection help you on your own journey through life.

My story began in West London, where I was born in the 1990s. Being the first son in a British-Pakistani household meant that I got away with a lot of mischief. Childhood was fun. I loved being outside and exploring, and my family afforded me a lot of freedom. Most days, I felt quite busy, my routine being: school, home, out with friends, back home to sleep.

Our formative early years have a lasting impact on us as we grow. In childhood, we first begin to appreciate beauty, ugliness, harm, and benefit, with colours appearing vivid, smells seeming fragrant, and the world seeming endless. One of my earliest childhood memories is of a warm sunny day, in which I remember the sun causing the world around me to glisten and warm. Birds were singing and the sky was blue—Allah, how magnificent!

I remember making friends for the first time. These other people—who moved and behaved like me—wanted to be around me. They wanted my company and valued me. We could explore the world together. It was fun.

Life's beauty and mystery can often distract you from its harsher realities and my earliest negative memory did not come until a while later. I remember seeing a rose when I was about 4 years of age. Curious and enchanted, I reached out to grab the stem, before being pricked firmly by the rose's thorn. I retracted my hand, and saw my bloodied hand, thinking it was the rose's petals which had coloured it, but I soon realised it was blood and began crying. It turned out that not every red thing was pleasant.

Life continues, despite the bumps along the way, and time is a powerful anaesthetic. We soon forget the occasional negative experience and move on to what will next please us. But life never stops sending us reminders and opportunities to reflect.

When I was 10 years old, I was out playing with my friends when I suddenly felt an intense pain in my chest. The pain was excruciating and it stopped me in my stride. Bent over, barely breathing, and overcome by a sense of panic, I felt, for the first time in my life that I was going to die. The pain soon passed, but I had no idea what had caused it. I suffered repeated bouts of similar, intense pain over the following weeks, moving in and out of hospital as a result. Vividly, I remember one occasion in which I was lying supine in the back of an ambulance, staring out of the window and thinking I may die very soon. My doctors found no anatomical cause of the pain and labelled it as a functional disorder related to irritable bowel syndrome. Accepting their diagnosis, I was relieved—functional neuropathy I can deal with; death I was not ready for.

I never forgot that period of my life. Life went on, but a Pandora's box of existential crises had now been opened. What followed were several years of soul-searching and introspection that led to the darkest point in my life.

As a teenager, I constantly asked myself questions I was unable to answer. Why was I alive? What is the purpose of life? What will happen after I die? My mortality was certain but everything else was unclear. Everyone who isn't completely subsumed into the grey sludge of modernity thinks about these things, but I felt I thought more than most. At times, I felt disconnected to the world around me, and often, I felt petrified at the thought of not being able to answer these questions in a way that would comfort me.

I began developing coping mechanisms, suppressing these questions the best I could and living in cognitive dissonance, one side of me unsure of anything and the other behaving as though the world really was meaningful. However, I could never fully suppress the questions, and each time they returned, they did so with increasing forcefulness. They would leave me feeling vulnerable, worn, and frustrated. A pattern began emerging—each subsequent time these questions arose, it took me longer to get back to normal life.

I was spiralling downwards.

CHAPTER 1
THE BLACK HOLE

One fateful evening, I rushed to my room upstairs and turned on my computer. It was my sanctuary and a place I could run to while away the hours of a long evening. This was during the early times of personal computers and my computer would constantly freeze or behave sluggishly, lacking behind my thoughts. I didn't mind—this was my time to think. My head space was becoming increasingly more occupied these days, and the moments of seclusion were cherished. Today, however, was different. I felt agitated and oddly sensitive. My emotions and senses were heightened.

As usual, my computer froze on me. This time I did mind. I lashed out, slamming my hands on the keyboard and cursing at the computer. I began striking the back of the computer like a madman. Something was not right.

I recall looking at the wall behind my computer and immediately being overcome by a powerful sense of self-awareness. I was aware that I was aware; I was conscious that I was conscious. It felt like I had just woken up from a dream, and that everything that had taken place in my life until that moment was illusory.

I glanced around the room. My emotions dimmed and emptiness crept in. I glanced around the room again. It all looked familiar but foreign. I rationalised to myself that the room was my own, where I had slept every night for the past years, but it felt like a completely new room. The emptiness and unease were persistent. I directed my attention to my own person, staring at my hands and trying to assure myself that I was not in an alternate reality. I couldn't recognise my hands. Again, I knew they were mine on a rational level, but I could not get them to feel like my own. It was as if I were looking at them properly for the first time in my life.

Peculiarly, my life had turned upside down internally, whilst the world around me remained unchanged. Any external observer would have found it odd that I was experiencing such a crisis. A cardiac arrest is witnessed and attested to by one's clinical markers, but this arrest of my spiritual heart was knowable only to me.

I left my room in an effort to extricate myself from the situation, hoping that a taste of the real world would rekindle normality. I left the house and started walking along the street on which I grew up. This street was meant to be familiar, with memories of friends and the hijinks we got up to in the past, but it no longer felt the same, and it felt as though I had entered an alien world.

To continue my search for familiarity, I ventured to my old friend's house. Seeing a familiar face would surely help. My friend opened the door and we stood there and spoke. Unlike me, he had had a completely normal day. The world held the same value in his mind as it had the previous day. In my mind, everything was now meaningless. The problem facing me now was: if all is meaningless, then so too are those people and places that I have long cherished. My friend is meaningless. My person is meaningless. My house is meaningless.

Humans innately find meaning in everything. We attach meaning to every individual, every moment, and everything around us. Our world has value to us. Extricating meaning and value from any item within the world bewilders us and feels unnatural. Suddenly, all that was sacred becomes material. They say that seeing the strings of the puppet at a puppet show snaps one out of the illusion of the moment. This occasion felt less like that and more like I had begun to see through the puppet altogether—neither string nor puppet seemed tangible anymore.

My world had become inescapably dark. The pessimism was all-consuming and left little room to hope, and though I was granted temporary respite from these moments throughout the ensuing days, the nihilism would soon return with vengeance. I was not able to normalise it either, as each moment of dread was both unpredictable and overwhelming. Between the moments of constriction my life was relatively normal, but I was not the same person mentally as I was before, even if I was still able to function. Then, when the dread overcame me, I felt paralysed.

I remember being in class at school and thinking, "Why am I in school?", "Why do I need an education?", "Why am I even alive?" These thoughts were relentless and exhausting, and the resultant fatigue became difficult to conceal in front of my friends. I tried to act as though all was fine, but I was internally torn to shreds. On my bad days, it was obvious something was wrong with me.

Obviously, this was not a normal state to be in. I kept trudging along in life, knowing that, for some reason, I had to carry on. I managed to convince myself that I had not gone mad, as a mad person—I told myself—was unaware of his own madness. I, on the other hand, was fully aware of the peculiarity of my state. I completely understood that something had gripped me internally and that I was unable to overcome it.

A series of seemingly unsurmountable existential questions were triggering a sense of anxiety within me and the lack of closure in my mind led to an appreciation of the world as inherently meaningless. This new worldview intensified my anxiety and torment, and it led to a disconnect between my conscious mind and everything else. What I did not know, however, was why a worldview in which the world seemed meaningless was a cause of such intense and acute pain.

My grasp of these moments of angst was incomplete. The issue which most concerned me was not completely clear to me. That being said, I knew that these feelings of dread were related some unresolved existential questions that plagued my mind. I just wanted it all to end.

The true nature of this pain, its cause, and its cure were not made clear to me until years later. Prior to this, I felt like a prisoner in my own mind, enshackled and unable to overpower his captor. The Hellenists used to believe that Prometheus had once stolen fire from heaven, leading Zeus to punish him through Pandora. He offered Pandora as a gift to Epimetheus, Prometheus' brother. Pandora was given a jar to safeguard, but curiosity led to her opening this jar, and out from it spilled sickness, death, and all the evils of the world. Though she rushed to quickly close the jar, the only thing she was able to save was 'hope'. The word for hope, in ancient Greek, can also mean deceptive expectation—a rather pessimistic outlook on what good remains on earth.

Recall our earlier mention of the power of storytelling and how the shared sufferings of humanity are expressed within stories. This legend reflects, in some way, what I was going through internally. Pandora was never able to bring back what she had let escape. Similarly, I felt as though, without external intervention, my situation would remain unresolved indefinitely.

Eventually, I realised I needed to speak to someone. This wasn't a one-man mission. But how could I tell my parents what I going through? Would they berate me? Chastise me? Consider me insane? Generally speaking, mental health is a taboo topic in Pakistani communities. Often, mental health conditions are seen as a façade for underlying sloth or weakness. Had this not been the case, I may have been able to approach someone sooner.

I mustered the courage to speak to my father. My father was a good man, one who was always there for his family financially, materially, and personally. He supported me throughout a hip operation I underwent as a child, keeping close to my side throughout the whole process and never wavering in his support of me. However, he was old-fashioned and not really very approachable for sentimental discussions.

Nervously, I told my father what was going on, not knowing how he would respond. Either he would understand my pain and see the human condition within me, or he would trivialise my pain and think of me as a weirdo. Without pausing for even a moment to breathe, I poured my heart out to my father. I unleashed the pain of those years of anguish and nihilism at his feet.

To my surprise, he was supportive. He did not berate me, nor did he trivialise my suffering. He empathised but averred that, in all his years of life, he had never come across such a situation before. He did not know what to say or do, but as a supportive father, he began to study common psychological ailments in an effort to aid me. Throughout the following years, my father never left my side, accompanying me to therapists and searching for the best doctors he could find to care for me.

Psychiatrists and clinical psychologists refer to what my condition was as a 'dissociative disorder', in which an individual loses contact with themselves and with the reality around them. Whether this matter is one of pathologising normality or there truly are chemical alterations that occur when one dissociates from the world is up for debate. How this condition occurs is well-studied; why this condition occurs is unknown. Why was I like this? Why did those questions torment me so?

By now, I was in my late teens, and the problem was not going away. I had been suffering for years and thought that, once I found answers to the deepest of my questions, all that was ailing me would disappear. However, whenever I searched to find answers, I hit dead ends. Dead ends are deeply discouraging phenomena. Pandora, in our earlier story, still held on to hope—a dead end makes one feel as though even hope is lost.

During periods in which my hope was lowest, I would try to suppress the problem through medication, drugs, or alcohol. I can still remember the first time I sought medical attention for my problem. I sat on a cold, hard, plastic chair in a dimly lit room beside my GP's office. That day was started out as one of my better days, as I was only experiencing a mild bout of anxiety and dissociation then. I felt somewhat optimistic, hoping to soon receive a cure.

"So, Mr Hussein, how may I help you?" asked the doctor. I wasn't sure what to tell him. Psychological complaints differ from medical ones. There is rarely any material evidence of a psychological predicament, no biomarkers to assist a clinician, and no objective clinical observations either. Nevertheless, I relayed everything I had been experiencing to the best of my ability.

The doctor paused before asking, "Have you taken any drugs?" "No," I replied, exhaling. He then averred a medical diagnosis, stating that I was suffering from a type of neurosis and needed to begin a course of antidepressants.

Antidepressants are numbing. They were not the answer to any of my questions, and those questions did not disappear when I took antidepressants. What the antidepressants did do, however, was make me somewhat apathetical to the situation. I cared less—not just about the questions that plagued me, but also about life in general. Everything was numb and flat. It became obvious that this was not a cure for my problem and my initial optimism of mine soon faded.

Alcohol soon became my secret repose. It numbed the pain, but it did not numb me entirely. I felt good when drunk; I felt happy. Pakistani Muslims, even those who do not practice Islam well, all know to avoid both alcohol and pork. At this point in my life, I did not care. As long as my family were unaware of my drinking habit, I was not concerned.

My local corner shop stored plenty of alcohol, and from there it was a short trip home before I would secretly take the drinks to my bedroom and begin drinking. I discovered the 'perfect' amount for me—not so much that I passed out, but enough to push all of my problems into the background. Alcohol allowed me to feel normal and to feel good. After drinking, I would have a few enjoyable hours of respite. The following day, I would repeat the process and all throughout day, I would be waiting for my evening drinking session and the pleasure that followed.

Deep down, I was aware of the self-destructive cycle I was entering. Alcohol was causing me more harm than benefit. I began to suffer from unhealthy eating habits, digestive problems, gastric ulcers, and gastric reflux. My physical health was being destroyed in an effort to save my mental health. And even my mental health was not receiving any lasting cures.

Fear began to set in. I was afraid that, if alcohol was not the answer, I would be out of solutions. I began to panic, which is not the best thing to do when you are trying to remedy dissociation and anxiety.

An alcohol addiction is a hard thing to overcome. Alcohol and I had an evidently toxic relationship. It led me to lonely walks in the streets at night, searching for another drink. I was suffering physically, and I knew my problems from before had not gone away. Oddly, looking up at the night sky on these lonesome walks gave me relief. The majesty of the night sky was not lost on me. I couldn't explain why, but looking up dwarfed all of my concerns, if only for a moment.

As I focused on what I saw, I began to appreciate that stars, despite being so extremely distant from one another, maintained their relative positions throughout the passing years. Every night, these stars would visit us and shine upon the earth with a sacred glow. They affirmed a certain order in the universe, and I, being a part of that same universe, must be governed by that same order.

My night walks were therapeutic. No longer was I seeing the world as a volatile mess of unshackled entropy that cantankerously trudged along void of purpose. Instead, I began to see control, determination, and meaning in life. The questions that had long tormented me must have answers, I thought. How could they not, when such majesty, beauty, and precision carpeted the night sky? How could all that be the result of unthinking entropy? And if the night sky has meaning, then so must I, for the night and I are of the same world.

It seemed impossible to me to think that human beings were no more than a composition of atoms. We were so obviously not only material beings. We had minds and consciousness—we know that about as well as we know anything at all. Denying it is not only audacious but delusional and self-defeating, as, without mind, we would have nothing to discard mind in the first place.

My thoughts continued. My experiences were real and I was existent, not just as a mass of carbon, but as a decision-maker, a thinker. The struggles in my mind were as real as my physical body. If anything, my experiences were as, or more, real than the observable world around me. If I were nothing more than a step in an evolutionary chain geared to survive and reproduce—two things which were of almost no concern to me at that point—then what explains the mind, thought, and the rest?

Inside me was something that was suffering. My body was mostly unscathed, but 'I' was suffering nonetheless. I realised that this 'I' was necessarily distinct from my physical body. It seems that this epiphany was not uniquely mine; it has been the concern of many philosophers throughout history.

In his book "Waking Up," Sam Harris argues that there is no 'I'. He avers that anyone searching for an I cannot locate it, meaning it is an illusion.[1] This argument is both self-defeating and based on two false premises. Firstly, if I am searching for an I, then I must exist. Further, to maintain that the 'I' that searches is a body and the 'I' that is sought is an illusion is a logical fallacy known as question-begging. Further still, the claim that that which cannot be localised must not exist cannot be taken for granted. There is no proof for this claim and it is counterintuitive to what our minds tell us.

It is clear why Sam Harris and those like him would claw at such easily dismissible arguments. Having a naturalistic, atheistic worldview necessitates that one denies anything other than the physical world. Accepting that anything non-physical could possibly exist opens up uncomfortable discussions for the atheist, discussions about the existence of God and the spirit.

Yet these atheists invest much of their time in trying to develop an alternative spirituality to what humanity has always resorted to—namely, religion. Though somewhat counterintuitive, it makes perfect sense to me why they do so. Spirituality and religion have always—without a single exception ever—been a part of human life. It is an inescapable part of our nature that can never be completely suppressed. Thus, they search for outlets to quench this thirst through, whilst paradoxically trying to maintain that their persons are nothing more than mindless, pre-determined collections of atoms.

Philosophers refer to this matter as the 'hard problem of consciousness'. What I am writing now is nothing new. No atheist ever solved the hard problem of consciousness; their attempts to deny that a problem exists in the first place has been fickle, as pointed out with an example above. One's consciousness, experience, and spirit cannot be measured in a test tube. It cannot be measured or dissected. A scientist could theoretically attach a patient to a monitoring device and hand him a bar of chocolate to taste. When the person tastes this chocolate, the monitoring device may well be able to track the movement and state of every nanoparticle within the patient's brain. However, none of this data can replicate the patient's experience when eating the chocolate. None of this explains what went on in their mind beyond the flavour and the dopamine spike.

In his book "The Divine Reality," Hamza Tzortzis discusses this issue at length. His conclusions, and the conclusion of most great thinkers who ever lived, is that something beyond the material world necessarily exists. Most of us are aware of this already, we intuitively understand that there is more to us than just our bodies.[2]

CHAPTER 2

EXISTENTIAL ANGST

Looking back at my childhood, all of these questions of life and its meaning were present very early on. All that happened over the years was that the questions became more refined and more prominent. Engaging my mind with these questions did make me feel a bit strange, but in truth, I was similar to most children in my behaviour and habits. To distract myself from these crippling thoughts, I would pick up hobbies whenever I could. At one point, I got into origami, buying multiple books on the subject and becoming somewhat skilled at the art.

Folding aeroplanes out of a sheet of paper amused me. How powerful is a mind that can wilfully take something so simple as plain paper and turn it into something so mechanically meaningful. I would study paper aeroplanes, learning which flourishes were purely aesthetic and which ones altered flight patterns.

One summer afternoon, I decided I would build an aeroplane with the longest flight pattern of any of the aeroplanes I had built thus far. The aim was to have as much hang time in the air as I could manage. I had done my research, and by now, I was adept at folding paper, knowing exactly how much pressure to apply with the tip of my nail for each fold. Each fold of mine was intentional and purposeful. I was confident that this aeroplane would outdo all previous ones I had constructed.

Once done, I beheld the most precisely constructed paper aeroplane I had ever made. The day outside was beautiful. It was a sunny day with perfect wind conditions for flight. The street was quiet—none of the usual children were out playing that day. The moment was opportune.

I walked to the middle of the road, paper aeroplane in hand, and begun to adjust the wings of my plane to optimise the angle. I scanned the environment keenly, one last time, to ensure that nothing would disrupt my mission. Then I threw the aeroplane. As soon as it left my hand, it adopted a life of its own, gliding magnificently through the air, banking left, as intended, before reaching its apex. At this point it felt as though time momentarily stopped.

The next 15 or so seconds felt like an eternity. They began with a sense of colossal achievement, my eyes fixed upon the flight path of my creation. The aeroplane had purpose, and it was fulfilling it, doing what it was created to do. Everything around me was similar—the trees, clouds, cars, and even the utility pole my aeroplane narrowly missed—they were all fulfilling a clear purpose. Then I began to wonder about myself. What was my purpose? And how am I supposed to fulfil that purpose?

Suddenly, that initial euphoria turned to emptiness. These thoughts had rushed through my mind in no more that 15 seconds. In such a short time, my 13-year-old mind went from appreciating the beauty of the world to feeling dread at my obliviousness to my purpose in life.

During these moments of my early life, it was as though I were trapped in a limbo of being, neither truly dead, nor truly living. My consciousness was real but was stagnant. My person was normal externally but hollow internally. My life was a binary one.

I eventually came to accept that wrestling with these questions was an integral part of being human. We all encountered such dilemmas. Some of us managed to suppress the thoughts through worldly engagements. Others managed to avoid thinking about them by focusing on material sciences. Others still must have been like me—in a constant search for truth. Every part of my being demanded answers. My frustration was due to me not having any.

Despite this, I was certain that answers existed, and I was confident that, upon seeing them, I would recognise them. It seemed self-evident to me that whilst these questions were present, so too was man's desire and ability to discover answers. At the time, I was unaware of what drove this urge, but soon I came to recognise it as an innate disposition within human nature.

Later in life, I came to realise that the anxiety and depression I had been suffering is what philosophers had long termed an 'existential angst'. Such an angst refers to the dread a human faces when he reflects upon his existence and sees himself as utterly insignificant due to a worldview that lacks any real answers to life's most important questions.

I realised my situation was not unique. What ailed me had ailed many before me. The intensity of my suffering had been felt by philosophers before me, and many philosophers had deemed suicide as the only viable option to escape from this predicament. They enquired whether life was worth living after they had deemed it naught but absurd. Such was their sorry state.

A group of philosophers who studied this problem became known as the existentialists. A core tenet of their school is the belief that humans are born without purpose and without meaning—in philosophical circles, this is typically phrased as being without 'essence'. These philosophers believed that, as free agents, humans must wander the earth and find their own purpose, giving their own lives meaning. Some existentialists—such as Søren Kierkegaard and Gabriel Marcel—believed in God, but most were atheists and naturalists.

Kierkegaard is widely considered to be the father of the existentialist school. Theistic and atheistic existentialist philosophers united upon the belief that existence preceded essence. In other words, they all believed that one was born without meaning and, thus, they needed to find meaning throughout their life. This same sentiment is affirmed by Jean-Paul Sartre in his book titled "Existentialism." He writes, "What they have in common is that they think that existence precedes essence, or, if you prefer, that subjectivity must be the starting point."[3]

Sartre was arguably the first to pen this core tenet of existentialist thought. He knew full well the implications of such a statement, and it troubled him greatly. Sartre was an atheist, and the sheer freedom his new formula afforded him was incredibly destabilising. Sartre did not believe in a God who gave meaning to the world. For Sartre, the world was godless and he could do anything he wished to do. All crime and sin seemed meaningless. All pain inflicted upon a vulnerable woman, child, or animal also seemed meaningless. In an effort to counter the havoc this would cause, Sartre, as other existentialist philosophers have subsequently done, paradoxically wrote extensively about living a 'responsible' life. Surely, the irony of what he was doing was not lost on him. Responsibility, and even encouraging good, is also meaningless—and it is not inherently better than its opposite—in an existentialist paradigm.

Naturalists are committed to the belief that everything can be explained through physical processes, and that nothing other than the physical world exists. Existentialism, atheism, and naturalism is a recipe for a bad curry. This combination lands one in a position from which it is impossible to answer any of life's major questions. Such a view necessitates that one believes in the world as a set of physical processes that lack intention, meaning, value, or purpose. To these people, everything is an accident, and no one accident is greater than another.

Philosophers refer to these individuals as existential nihilists. Nihilism is the belief that meaning does not exist. Such an outlook can destroy a man—man's whole being yearns for answers and his worldview tells him to stop searching and to close his eyes as all he intuits is illusory. For this reason, Albert Camus and others scoff at the existential nihilist's notion of searching for meaning whilst believing that meaning does not truly exist—an absurdity.[4] Camus came to accept that life without God was meaningless, but he maintained that suicide was not the solution. Instead, he famously claimed that the literal meaning of life was "whatever you're doing that prevents you from killing yourself."[5]

Philosophers still discuss and debate the true meaning of life. Largely, they are divided into four camps:

1. those who believe that there can be no meaning without God;

2. those who believe that a belief in God can enhances one's life by giving it more meaning;

3. those who believe that one can have a perfectly meaningful life without God; and

4. those who argue that a belief in God removes meaning from one's life.

Reflecting on these four groups made me appreciate that objective meaning can only be found through God. Any godless world must necessarily be either meaningless or have a meaning that is conjured by will and whim—and any meaning that is conjured by will or whim must be inherently subjective. "Surely, it is in the remembrance of God that hearts find peace."[6]

Before my existential crises, I would not have described myself as an atheist or a naturalist. Rather, I would have considered myself an agnostic who was not concerned either way. What I was certain of was the existence of a world around me. Beyond this world, I had no belief in another. I never felt a need to deny the existence of a creator, but neither did I feel a need to affirm this claim. It made complete sense that a God would exist, but I never felt that this was linked to my own personal life. My state was one akin to that of Kierkegaard— though he was a stronger Christian than I was a Muslim—and other existentialists, atheists or otherwise. This is how I approached life's big mysteries.

Were I to hazard a guess, I'd say there are many people who grow up in such a state of mind in our postmodern world. Our world is focused almost exclusively on a horizontal plane, with its endless material distractions and all-consuming competitions. We spend countless hours on social media, on online shopping websites, socialising, and toiling away at work. An ideal life in the eye of a postmodern man is one in which he accumulates as much material comfort as he can.

The enlightenment thinkers sold humanity a new vision in the 18th century, a vision in which the purpose of man was to create a utopia upon earth. What ensured was a materialism and consumerism that consumed us. In "The High Price of Materialism," Tim Kasser avers that materialism's centrality within our life has eroded both our relationships and our lives themselves.[7] Further still, we seem to have lost the balance of consumption and restraint, of giving and taking, of moving and pausing.

How such an existence keeps one distracted from metaphysical thought is clear. How it pushes one into a naturalistic understanding of the world is also clear. Couple this with an exaggerated conception of the scientific method and we have the state of a postmodern atheist.

Every human must, however, even if only on occasion, have moments of deeper thought and realisation. In those moments, the existentialist necessarily ponders life's big questions. He compares his first-person subjective experience with the worldview he has unthinkingly adopted. When he realises that the latter entails that the former is meaningless, a sense of dread and emptiness sets in. Were he to persist upon this train of thought, his existential angst would spiral into existential depression. This was how my crisis began.

Some existentialists tried to sidestep this pain with a more positive view of their state of mind. They averred that, without a defined purpose, a human finds endless possibilities. He is empowered to become whatever he wishes to, and he chooses his own purpose. Sartre was one such philosopher. He wrote, "Man is nothing else but what he makes of himself. Such is the first principle of existentialism. It is also what is called subjectivity, the name we are labelled with when charges are brought against us. But what do we mean by this, if not that man has a greater dignity than a stone or table? For we mean that man first exists, that is, that man first of all is the being who hurled himself towards a future and who is conscious of imagining himself as being in the future. Man is at the start a plan which is aware of itself, rather than a patch of moss, a piece of garbage, or a cauliflower; nothing exists prior to this plan; there is nothing in heaven; man will be what he will have planned to be."[3]

For Sartre, it is human consciousness that distinguishes humans from other material objects. He held that the human capacity to will and plan a future gave us value. Sartre was aware of how these claims equated sin with virtue, murder with cure, and torture with charity. After all, what stopped someone from deciding that causing intense suffering was good, and that it was their purpose? Why should it be so that only what most people want is valid as a purpose? Sartre, thus, wrote heavily on responsible living in an effort to mitigate this.

However, these coping mechanisms are fickle. Humans have a way to alter their perception of reality to make things seem less depressing than they are, but this pseudo-positive existential philosophy does not stand up to even a slight degree more of scrutiny. An existentialist believes that meaning does not exist; then he wishes to believe that meaning is that which he imparts upon a matter—the contradiction is clear. If there is no value or purpose, no good or evil, then your subjective judgements of good and evil are in no way objective or true. They are only meaningless, valueless, purposeless, opinions—and all opinions are is a predetermined interchange of neurons in a mass of randomly configured carbon that forms a body. Hardly dignified.

One day, many years ago now, I walked past a butcher shop and saw many carcasses of sheep and cows hanging just behind the shop window. I paused to reflect. In the glass window, I could see my own reflection, and beyond it, I could see the row of carcasses. These carcasses were bloodless and lifeless. They had muscles and fibres, bones and skin.

Not long before, these carcasses would have been living beings with blood gushing through their veins and neurotransmitters running through their minds. Once they had lost life, they were no longer considered animals—they were now a carcasses. I wondered what had changed between the two states, and I wondered what had differentiated me from the carcass if we were only physical processes devoid of meaning. Death was no tragedy in a meaningless world, it was only the continuation of the same physical processes that preceded it, none being more important than the other.

Innately, we place value on everything. In the material world, we value human life more than the lives of others, and we value the lives of other species more than we do non-sentient matter. Secular struggles with this self-evident truth have led to modern movements such as humanism and the committee for human rights.

Again, however, these movements are logically inconsistent coping methods that do not stand up to scrutiny. In an atheistic worldview, there is no logical compulsion whatsoever to value human life and freedom over anything else. If a human is nothing but matter, then does he really matter? And if he does not matter, then why not kill him if it pleases you? No special significance and value can be given to life—as opposed to death—and so no one can say a murderer or rapist has done any real wrong—wrong does not truly exist in this worldview, after all.

The logical conclusion of existential atheism is that a human life has no more value that an inanimate object. As one does not care when he steps on a blade of grass, so he need not care if he were to step on the face of his fellow man.

People often clutch at straws to square an atheistic worldview with a moralistic one. They use arguments such as those that claim our value stems from our 'complexity' or our 'sentience'. However, none of this is substantiated from any first principles in an atheistic worldview. None of these arguments logically necessitate, or even suggest that life has value. Atheists all live in cognitive dissonance, and their populist proponents try tirelessly to pretend otherwise. So many arguments against theism, and religion in general, stem from loosely adopted moral stances—none of this holds up to scrutiny when you realise that atheism necessitates pure and unfettered moral relativity.

My own struggle with existential angst led to me seeking counselling and psychotherapy. My therapist asked me how I wanted to feel, and I immediately replied, "Happy!" My greatest wish was to be happy again, like I was when I was a child and out playing with my friends. The world was beautiful back then, and there was so much yet to explore.

I maintained a façade of composure in front of my therapist, but internally, I was in tears. What I had lost in terms of youthful bliss had already passed. I was more concerned with moving on and getting past this stage. The life ahead of me was going to pan out in one of two ways—nihilism or serenity. It's not that I never had happy moments. There were many, many occasions in which I felt a sense of happiness and joy, but these were invariably followed by misery and nothingness, and then the questions on my mind would always return.

Many people identify life's purpose as achieving maximal happiness. Our innate disposition is one that runs towards felicity. For spiritually inclined Muslims, this has often been understood as a yearning for Eden and proximity to the divine. During my existential angst, I was agnostic and unconcerned with God. Therefore, to my mind, happiness was as meaningless as the things I was occasionally happy about. For the theist, happiness is meaningful, not in a wishy-washy subjective way, but truly meaningful. I was not experiencing that level of happiness.

Some humans are, perhaps, able to suppress these questions and distract themselves in the world. They aren't concerned with truths and ultimate reality. Rather, they understand that they exist, that some things give them joy, and that they wish to pursue those things that give them joy. The deeper questions are drowned under the sound of commerce and play. I felt unable to do this. I wanted to know the truth.

Hamza Tzortzis, in his book "The Divine Reality," mentions the following, "While reading this, you are sedated against your will. Suddenly you wake up and find yourself on a plane. You're in first class. The food is heavenly. The seat is a flatbed, designed for a luxurious, comfortable experience. The entertainment is limitless. The service is out of this world. You start to use all of the excellent facilities. Time starts to pass. Now think for a moment, and ask yourself the question: Would I be happy? How could you be? You would need some questions answered first. Who sedated you? How did you get on the plane? What is the purpose of the journey? Where are you heading? If these questions remained unanswered, how could you be happy? Even if you started to enjoy all of the luxuries at your disposal, you would never achieve true, meaningful happiness. Would a frothy Belgian chocolate mousse on your dessert tray be enough to drown out the questions? It would be a delusion, a temporary, fake type of happiness, only achieved by deliberately ignoring these critical questions."[2]

Hamza captured the human condition so well. In his scenario, all the pleasures one could think of are available to the person. But without meaning, and without knowing the truth, and without a connection with something higher, this person will not be at ease.

During my time at university, I managed to distract myself from the persistent questions. Alcohol was still present in my life, but what was once an addiction was now only a social habit. I moved out of my paternal home during my second year of university, and this new freedom and excitement numbed my existential angst. I did not have enough free time to be overly concerned with existential questions. Eventually, I became convinced that my old state was just that—something in the past.

I became a happy person, but that person was not my real self. It was an avatar of sorts that I had intentionally sculpted in an effort to sidestep what ailed me. There's a reason computer games and social media are so addictive among people of all ages. In past years, the postmodern man sought to establish meaning through a moral life, even when he did not really believe in morals truly existing. Nowadays, nihilism has been embraced with open arms. What we have done to cope with this is produce alternative projections of reality. Escapism refers to the tendency to find distractions in an effort to avoid unpleasant realities. We have become escapists living through avatars that have game-based rules and order. Meanwhile, we lose our own connection with the real world that we live in.

One evening in university, I was sat with some friends, drinking alcohol and smoking, as we would do every night, and we were joking and laughing about the day's events. I had everything I wanted from the material world: good friends, a good education, and value and acceptance within my social circle. It felt good. I was happy. And then the thoughts suddenly returned. Who were these people? Why did their companionship matter? What is the purpose of a good education?

Around me the conversation was continuing. Internally, I was in turmoil again. Those good feelings I had just experienced had left me by now and I was just trying to maintain composure in the room. The emptiness gave way to despair. I was never the same again thereafter, avoiding contact with my friends as much as possible. Being around people seemed meaningless and fake, and I wasn't willing to pretend anymore.

The academic year came to a close and I was returning home broken. Medical therapy, psychotherapy, drugs, alcohol, and socialising had all failed me. My options were running out. During the summer, I remained locked in my room and began my old routine again. I would comfort eat to numb the pain and buy a 50 cl bottle of spirit to drink every evening.

The mere thought of returning to university to see my friends again brought upon panic and a bolt of anxiety was felt passing through my spine. I was anhedonic, no longer finding pleasure in what previously gave me joy. At the forefront of my mind were those fatal questions; nothing else was of significance to me.

Reluctantly, I returned to university for my third year. Weighing 20 lbs more than when I left, I was now, visibly, a changed man. I decided to live at home and commute into university, as this meant I did not need to face my flatmates every day. Despite this, I wasn't able to avoid my classmates. My best friend at the time was a man named Sam. He immediately noticed the weight gain but also that I was hiding a deeper problem. During lunch on the first day back, he walked me outside the block and sat me down, asking, "What's wrong? You don't seem like yourself."

I hesitated in my response. Till now, Sam had known me as a normal person, just like the rest of our friend circle. He was fond of me, and I had never disclosed my existential angst to any of my friends. Not wanting him to deem me mad, I stayed silent for a while, had a think, and then said, "I've just been feeling low—a little depressed. But I don't know why—I've just been thinking about the meaning of life." Sam paused for a few moments, then looked me in the eye and said, "You know, I felt like that too, once. I had broken up with my girlfriend and was really depressed for a while. During that time, I, too, questioned the purpose of my life—but then I just got on with it and forgot about it."

I wasn't sure what to make of his advice. Was he being dismissive of my pain and telling me to just move on? Was his scenario very different to mine and so any comparison not really fair? Or was I just overanalysing a simple gesture of kindness from a friend? Whatever the case, I wore my avatar smile and walked back to class with him. We never spoke of this again.

As my final year at university progressed, I began to think that, perhaps, the answers to my questions lay in a realm beyond the physical one I was accustomed to. By now, I had concluded that materialism and naturalism were neither going to provide me with answers, nor were they going to cure my angst.

Throughout my time at university, I realised that many people suffered from bouts of depression every now and again. Some of my closest friends went through rough periods on occasion. Each person seemed to be trying to fill the void within them with money, education, friends, and companionship. Invariably, these endeavours would fail people, or those people would lose interest and move on to the next quick fix. In many ways, my unease was felt by them, too—they just weren't as conscious of it as I was.

CHAPTER 3

SPIRITUAL TRUTHS IN AN AGE OF MATERIALISM

My drinking habits and overeating were taking a toll on my physical health. My digestive issues had returned, and I had gained considerable weight. Broken externally and internally, I felt it was time to finally give up. For the first time in my life, I lashed out at a God I did not know existed. I cried out, "Why me? Why are you doing this to me?" My anger and desperation had peaked.

Before this point in my life, I do not recall ever speaking to God—I had never felt the need to. For the past seven years, I had tried everything I could to escape my dilemma, and now I stood a broken and humbled man. My plea to God was unplanned. It was a visceral response to a psychospiritual phenomenon. Perhaps this is common among humans. When we are truly broken-hearted and have lost trust in this lowly world, we face upwards towards the heavens and cry out to a deity, seeking help.

This action of mine was not something I could rationalise. All I knew is I needed help. I continued to scream at God, asking Him for answers, asking for signs. I received no answer and eventually stopped calling. There was an odd silence in the room and an unusual sense of stillness, but nothing else—my angst remained. Nothing had changed, and then I fell asleep, not knowing how pivotal this moment would prove to be in my life to come.

Upon waking, I had developed a peculiar interest in world religions. For some reason, I was not interested in Islam at this point. Instead, I investigated Christianity, Hinduism, Sikhism, and other religions. My avoidance of Islam was, most likely, due to the negative experiences I had with Muslims growing up. Further, as I grew up in a Muslim family, I assumed I knew about Islam already.

I continued studying these religions for months. I was contemplative during this time, often going for walks and speaking into the ether, asking questions and not receiving verbal answers. Never did I see a bolt of lightning or a parting sea, but I was not left alone either. I would repeatedly see signs in the world around me, very subtle signs, but ones that appeared very direct and very intentional.

I began to study the language of signs, wanting to know how to interpret what I was witnessing. I was being spoken to, and I needed to pay attention. My search into world religions continued unsatisfactorily, and I was left without a religion that seemed correct. It felt as though I were a climber trying to escape a crevice into which I had fallen. As I ascended, I would reach a limit beyond which nothing to cling onto remained. I would then descend and try to climb in a different location. The sequence would repeat itself multiple times as I searched through religions.

One roadblock I kept facing was that the religions I studied had no satisfactory link between God and the purpose of man. Those religions that did seem to offer a purpose for man did not have acceptable conceptions of God—and my reason, intuition, and experiences would not let me accept aberrant conceptions. Those religions that had more rational understandings of God did not seem to offer logically satisfying reasons for the purpose of man.

Christianity averred a trinitarian doctrine in which one part of a three-pronged godhead was sent down to earth in an act of both suicide and deicide. This seemed hugely problematic to me, and in no way did it concur with reason. Hinduism pushed a polytheistic worldview in which a higher god is accompanied by lesser ones. This, too, seemed counterintuitive and unnecessary.

Sifting through religions to find the truth can be frustrating—as it was for me back then—and I can see why atheists often use this frustration as a reason to abandon religion altogether. I've come across logical fallacies such as, "There are so many religions, each with a different god or different gods. This means no one must have the answer." This argument is dismissible from a purely logical standpoint—there may be 100 theories on who shot JFK, but that does not mean that JFK was never actually shot [though some people believe he wasn't]. However, the argument also overlooks a powerful truth I came across: yes, each religion had a different understanding of what it meant to be a deity, but every religion I came across had a common theme—they all accepted that an omnipotent creator existed. Nobody rejected this.

I was far from being a theologian, and far from wanting to become one. All I wanted was answers to the questions I had. For the first time in my life, I felt that I was looking in the right direction to find answers. One fateful afternoon, I noticed a copy of the Qur'ān sat atop a shelf near me. I had seen it before throughout the years, but never paid it much attention. It felt new. I began to think that, perhaps, I did not really know what Islam was, and that maybe I should read this book. Whilst feeling an urge to read, I felt a stronger urge to avoid it. There was a sense of arrogance in my attitude to Islam, I felt it was not worth looking into. Despite this, the more I avoided it, the more I found it in front of me.

Eventually, I gave in to my curiosity and thought I should at least give Islam a chance. I picked up the Qur'ān and was surprised by how little I actually knew of this religion. The more I read, the more I wanted to continue reading. It was astonishing to me that I had read this book in Arabic—a language I don't understand—during my childhood without ever appreciating what was being said. The experience was bizarre; this book was explaining so many things perfectly. I did not come across naturalistic miracles like the ones I had been asking for previously, I came across something more powerful: life's questions were being answered.

The books author described Himself and I felt as though I knew Him already. Chapter 112 of the Qur'ān reads:

"Say, 'He is God, the One!

God the Eternal Sustainer.

He begetteth not nor was begotten.

And there is none comparable unto Him.'"[8]

I had never read this and understood it before. It affirmed all my intuitions and aligned with reason. God is singular, unique, unchanging, and independent. This made rational sense and appeared to concord with the guiding hand I had been experiencing recently. My stubbornness meant I refused to believe in anything Islamic just yet, but I was beginning to open up to studying more.

As I read the Qur'ān, I repeatedly reached sentences which felt as if they were addressing my current moment. Other sentences seemed to address my agony over the past seven years.

"What was my purpose?" I wondered. "I created the jinn and humankind only that they might worship Me."[9] God answered.

"Who am I?" I asked. "Surely We created man of the best stature..."[10] God stated, saying elsewhere, "Truly we have honoured the Children of Adam. We carry them on the land and the sea, and have made provision of good things for them, and have preferred them above many of those whom We created with a marked preferment."[11]

"What is the point of this world existing?" I thought. God informed us, "Exalted is He who holds all control in His hands; who has power over all things; who created death and life to test you [people] and reveal which of you does best—He is the Mighty, the Forgiving..."[12]

"Where am I going?" I enquired. God said, "Lo! those who believe and do good works, for them are the gardens of delight..."[13] and, "Say [O Muhammad] unto those who disbelieve, 'Ye shall be overcome and gathered unto Hell, an evil resting-place.'"[14]

Whatever questions I had, they were all being answered through the Qur'ān. The actual Qur'ān is in Arabic—the English 'translations' aren't perfect, but they were all I could rely on at the time. Even then, something so profound and transformative was taking place within me. We were created to worship God. Worship in the Qur'ān seemed to be so much more than unthinking, dogmatic, submission to rituals and tradition. Kindness to neighbours, to parents, and to the enfeebled was all worship. Charity was worship. Prayer was worship. Defending the truth with your body on the line was worship. Yes! This was all worship.

And regarding submission and lowering oneself—my worry was that religion would cage me and turn me into an unfree man. But that was not what I found in the Qur'ān. As a supposedly free man before these unveilings, I was enshackled by whichever vice, fad, or impulse I was dealing with at the time. I read in my translation of the Qur'ān, "Have you seen the one who takes as his god his own desire? Then would you be responsible for him?"[15] This was describing me! Submission to something, whether one believes it to be innate disposition, or evolutionary instincts, or psychosocial ideals, or voluptuary lusts, or mechanical forces is necessary—why not submit, instead, to God? This was the epiphany I had. Through submission to God, one finds liberation from all else.

What also struck me was the concept of life being a testing ground before we move on to a more permanent abode. People often struggle with a concept of God due to the chaotic and, at times, cruel nature of some of what happens within the world. It perplexes many a mind that the universe is so perfectly sculpted yet we see injustice and haphazardness in the world around us. This makes little sense unless we appreciate the passing nature of the present and the infinite nature of the abode to come.

The Qur'ān also made it clear that life did not end at the grave, and that the soul continued onwards after our material death. Life was consequential, and our actions would have repercussions in the life to come. In view of this, I introspected on how I had lived my life up until now. I had suffered through immense mental torture for seven years, and it brought me to this path. "Was it worth it?" I wondered. "If this was the truth…" I thought, "then it is worth all the pain in the world." As the sufferings of the first world are washed over with the bliss of the abode to come, so too would my past pain be repaid with extreme generosity. But I still needed more convincing.

Rationally, things were falling into place—I was being slowly convinced. Everything made sense. However, my heart was not ready to accept Islam as a religion. I wondered what could have been the wisdom behind my being depressed for the past seven years, and then I came across the following from the Qur'ān, "But he who turns away from remembrance of Me, his will be a depressed life, and I shall bring him blind to the assembly on the Day of Resurrection."[16]

The message was not despondent, however, and chances for a return to the felicity of youth and beyond were made available, "O mankind! There hath come unto you an exhortation from your Lord, a healing for that which is in the breasts, a guidance and a mercy for believers."[17] Any grief which warns a man on the brink of destruction and guides him to salvation is grief he is thankful for—one's pain immediately turns to pleasure.

Every claim being made was turning out to be true. Everything was making sense. As I continued reading, the coherence and consistency became increasingly apparent. My soul was torn, a part of it convinced and a part of it still doubtful. How was this the case, when what I was experiencing was a book that was engaging with me beyond a mere rational level? Knowing a fire burns without ever having come into contact with it is not the same as having the flames licking one's naked skin and then appreciating the heat. It is hard to forget the latter experience.

Though having touched this metaphorical flame, I still harboured some reservations. It is hard to pin down exactly why this was the case. As human beings, we get comfortable in certain surroundings and our minds get comfortable in certain paradigms. We become used to seeing the world in a certain way, and anything that tries to drastically change that makes us uncomfortable. Personally, I used to see the world in a purely secular light, and now a book had reached me that was explaining a purely sacralised world. This made me uncomfortable.

There was something more that lay behind my reluctance. Through-out schooling, university, and growing up in general, I had been conditioned to seeing the world through a notion of 'seeing is be-lieving'. It is not as if someone ever sat me down and said, "This is how you will now see the world." It happened more orgnaically and through a secularised mechanistic approach to everything around me. Leaving this paradigm was uncomfortable—could there really exist something beyond what I could see, hear, smell, touch, or taste?

Beyond this conundrum, I realised that, were I to accept what this book was calling me to, then I would have had to give up a number of habits that I had developed in life. Some of these changes would be drastic. Mentally, I was not prepared for such a change, especially as my life had already been so chaotic and unbalanced recently.

Often, we avoid facing hard truths—hard, both because they aren't mouldable into something we want them to be and because they can tear through the mental façades we previously held on to so dearly. Our intellect may be able to see something as the truth but our lower self strives its utmost not to accept it. As I was reading my transla-tion of the Qur'ān, I came across the following, "I shall turn away from My revelations those who magnify themselves wrongfully in the earth, and if they see each sign believe it not, and if they see the way of righteousness choose it nor for [their] way, and if they see the way of error choose if for [their] way. That is because they have denied Our signs and paid them no heed."[18]

At this point in my life, it was as if I was stood atop a tightrope, with a pool of belief on one side and a pool of disbelief on the other. I was seeing so many signs, so many things were being answered, but I had my reservations. There was a cognitive dissonance with which I lived, and this phase lingered for a few weeks.

One day, whilst walking along a road, I began reflecting on my life, the darkness I had experienced, and how hopeless I felt. I decided to pick up a copy of the Qur'ān and read something from its translation. This was something I had begun doing regularly when I felt distressed. With a sense of dread within me, I randomly opened up Chapter 113 of the Qur'ān. It was titled, "The Daybreak." The first sentence read, "Say, 'I seek refuge in the Lord of the Daybreak.'"[19]

There was silence. I wanted a new day to break through in my life. The darkness of the long night had become overwhelming. I was being spoken to through this book again. Spoken to directly. For some reason, I needed to pause before reading on. My translation of the Qur'ān came with additional commentary, and I looked to find the commentary on this sentence. It read, "[Falaq] is the Dawn or Day break, the cleaving of the darkness and the manifestation of light. This may be understood in various senses: [1] literally, when the darkness of the night is at its worst, rays of light pierce through and produce a new dawn; [2] when the darkness of ignorance is at its worst, the light of Allah [God] pierces through the soul and gives it enlightenment."[20]

It is incredibly hard to explain just how powerful this moment felt. Not only were my thoughts being responded to, but I was also literally experiencing what was being described. My heart burst open, and like a daybreak, a sense of peace, comfort, and light burst through, embracing me. I felt comfort and love like I had not felt before, and it was at this moment that I was convinced that this was the truth, without any doubt.

Sat on the ground with tears flowing from my eyes, I was overcome with a gratitude and peace that filled my heart. My heart had recognised the truth and it had accepted it.

God said, "Then, even after that, your hearts were hardened and became as rocks, or worse than rocks, for hardness. For, indeed, there are rocks from which rivers gush, and, indeed, there are rocks which split asunder so that water flows from them. And, indeed, there are rocks which fall down from the fear of Allah. Allah is not unaware of what you do."[21]

Discussing and acknowledging metaphysical realities is no mean feat in an age of materialism, mechanism, and Epicureanism. I know this, as I was one of those who resisted until the last moment. Our world is full of sensual pleasures and distractions. It is bejewelled with beautiful embellishments throughout its land and seas. It is enchanting and distracting, and one risks losing the wood for the trees, for lack of a better metaphor, if they indulge unthinkingly within the world. One may also fall into a superficial sense of fulfilment and independence, losing track of their inner selves. Any truth that lies beyond the material is dismissed as nothing more than a fairy tale.

Spirituality is a forgotten subject today. More than that—it is a despised subject in most conversations. Anything that is not physical is ignored or hated by people. People do not have any evidence why something non-physical cannot exist, but they hold on to that belief with fervour. If you wish to begin a discussion about metaphysics, you often have to accept being seen as an outcast by the unbelievers in our world.

However, it needn't be this way. Almost every philosopher in history has appreciated metaphysics in their studies. Science was once seen as a range of subjects, such as mathematics [being qua numbers] and natural philosophy [being qua matter; what we now call science], that sat underneath the subject of metaphysics [being qua being]. It is only a recent phenomenon that we don't study religious truths anymore in mainstream discourse. Our busy lives, shifting paradigms, and arrogance preclude us from an honest reading of religion.

Our language, culture, intuition, and reason belie this aversion, however. Examples of linguistic and cultural references to the spiritual heart and soul include, "It touched my heart," "She has a big heart," "From the bottom of my heart," "Let's just have a heart-to-heart," "You broke my heart," "He has lost his soul," and "He is soul-searching." The list is long, and it stems from an ancient connection to what we know feel but try to cover up. At some point in our lives, we have all felt something spiritual, something that touched our hearts. Some feel it almost viscerally, and to the spiritually attuned, it can be clearer than a physical touch. If one forces a physical-only paradigm upon their understanding, then, of course, nothing beyond the physical will be easily accepted. But when we appreciate that this paradigm is a choice, and is in no way provable, then a world of possibilities opens up—our minds become unshackled and we become able to think more freely.

After my experience with the Qur'ān, everything changed. The world seemed different. Things were now more vivid, more beautiful, and more clear. Everything made sense, including my own self. That being said, I had some lingering pain, anxiety, and PTSD from my former state. Psychological trauma does not usually vanish in an instant. Yet I still felt a peace and comfort I had not known before, and I learned how to heal. I learned at this time of the great worship of turning to God for your needs. God had not created and abandoned us—He is near. God said, "Pray unto Me and I will hear your prayer."[22]

Whenever we call upon God, he answers in line with his perfect wisdom. I decided to call and seek his advice. At this time in my life, I was trying to learn how to perform the five daily prayers in Islam. I had forgotten everything I knew as a child and had to start from the beginning. It was not easy, but I was determined. One day, I fell into prostration out of submission to God and a love of Him. Curiously, this was the practice also of the Prophet Jesus [upon him be peace]. We find the following in the Bible, "Going a little further, he fell with his face to the ground and prayed, 'My Father, if it is possible, may this cup be taken from me. Yet not as I will, but as you will.'"[23]

During this prostration, I beseeched God with earnest zeal to help me—He was the One who knew all and controlled all. In my prayer, I asked God to remove these darker emotions from me and to replace them with what was my normal state from before. I implore you to not accuse me with exaggeration when I say the following: the moment I raised my head, all my negative emotions had left. Whatever had plagued me for seven years vanished in an instant. I searched for those feelings and still could not find them within me. This was nothing short of a miracle—what else could I honestly call it? My heart tasted the certainty of faith.

Allah says, "He it is Who sent down peace of reassurance into the hearts of the believers that they might add faith unto their faith. Allah's are the hosts of the heavens and the earth, and Allah is ever Knower, Wise..."[24]

CHAPTER 4

FREEDOM IN SUBMISSION

Getting a job as a design engineer during a British recession which hit London very hard was a blessing and a relief. I was soon back in the hustle and bustle of life and on track to receive everything a man could reasonably ask for: education, a good job with room to progress, a nice car, a big house, a wife, kids, and a healthy pension. For some reason, however, my soul wished to rebel against these ideals of living.

Every morning, I rode the London Underground to commute to work. As the train moved centrally, more and more working professionals would board, dressed to impress and ready to face the working day ahead. Some would be engrossed in their phones, others would read, and others still would try their utmost to focus on anything other than a stranger's face lest a conversation begin. I hated the commute, but it didn't seem like I had much of a choice, so it was a chore I just got on with.

It was actually on one of these commutes that I had an epiphany about human psychology. Every human being I saw was a slave to one thing or another. Just like myself, these professionals were doing what they were told would yield the aforementioned ideal life. They likely spent years of studying and hard work to get to where they were now. Yet the cold faces I saw in front of me were not radiant and fulfilled. My own face that would stare back at me in the train's window was similarly joyless. It hit me then that we were all enslaved whether we knew it or not.

Historically, an enslaved person was easy to identify through their dress, speech, or treatment. Lines were clear back then. In the 21st century, we have a softer form of the same thing. We aspire to freedom and are sold it through advertising, but in reality, we are lured to traps which consume us and distract us from our true joys and true purpose in life. We feel free as we accumulate more, but our freedom should really have been found in not needing to accumulate more and in being able to look upwards towards the heavens in awe and wonderment. Instead, most of us spend the best hours of our lives feeding pharaohs that sit atop financial pyramids.

Tim Kasser argues that one's degree of adherence to materialist values is inversely proportional to their degree of adherence to social values.[7] His research led him to conclude that, as we become more materialistic, we care less about forming and maintaining meaningful relationships and spending time with family and friends. Further, when our self-definition and the valuation of our self-worth is determined through material wealth, rates of mental disorders and low self-esteem rise.[7] It seems largely intuitive that, when our worth is considered to be that which is outwith our person, then what is within our person is afforded less meaning and value.

During my early commutes, my fellow passengers deemed themselves free, just as I used to. However, they were couped into the train to be shuttled to offices to work for another person for most of their useful waking hours. Most of their remaining hours, when bosses relieved them of duties, was spent mindlessly consuming digital content and attending social functions as proscribed. This cycle would repeat until their economic worth declined in their old age, and then they would be released and considered a 'burden' on a society 'struggling' with an ageing population. Death would then take them and all their accumulated wealth would be taken by others.

If this is the case, why is the accumulation of wealth considered a measure of value. Why do we even care? Yes, earning a living and being productive in the world are important matters, but anything material should not be considered our main priorities. We should not delude ourselves into thinking we behave as we do for a higher ideal when our behaviour proves the opposite.

Those who feel that they are not consumed by the compulsive forces of our post-industrial system and only follow their own wishes are often even less free, acting on impulse, whim, and as a slave to the base desires they have lost control of. An impulse must be behind any of our actions—something even the early Greek philosophers understood to be a logical necessity—and this impulse is what enslaves us. Blessed is he whose impulse is to serve a benevolent God.

Submission to God entails that we acknowledge Him as the only being worthy of worship. We accept our intrinsic powerlessness and that to God belongs the dominion of the heavens and the earth. This maxim is immensely cathartic and relieves one of all the stress in the world. No longer does one need to depend on any living creature or any material thing. He begins to see through the creation, beyond it, to something deeper.

God is omnipotent, unfailing, unflinching, and most kind. Reliance on him is not like reliance on a creation that cannot sustain itself or even understand the true nature of its own situation. Once we accept the reality of things as they are, we become able to submit to God and free ourselves from the world. This is true freedom.

At this point in my life, I had accepted God and submitted myself to him, but this newfound freedom felt uncomfortable. It was unusual to see the world in this way. As I grew closer to God, things became increasingly clear, and I felt increasingly free. The opinion of others mattered less to me. I became less arrogant. I became more loving. I began to overflow with joy and see purpose in the world around me, in the people around me, including both my friends and my enemies. Oddly, I felt closer to the world, not more distant, even though I had renounced it. Some spiritual wayfarers stress a principle of 'khalwah dar anjuman' [seclusion in company]. One can be wholly present with the people, 'ibn al-waqt' [a son of the moment], making the utmost of the moment he finds himself in, whilst being secluded from them and wholly belonging to God. The beauty and joy of this state is difficult to put into words.

God is not only the creator, but he is the all-powerful sustainer of creation. Every moment, every movement, and every matter is under his sovereignty. This sacred worldview liberated me from my compulsion to appease the whims of people. My purpose was higher, and I now understood that my benefitting the people was itself an act of worship to God, and not the result of my submission to creation.

God says, "Say, He is Allah, One! Allah the eternal. He begets not, nor was begotten. And there is none comparable unto Him."[25] This is a translation of the entire 112th chapter of the Qur'ān. The chapter is referred to as the Chapter of al-Ikhlāṣ [Sincerity]. Here, God is described as aḥad, a word which means he is singular, alone, indivisible, and not a part of anything else. The next sentence is two-words-long, "Allahu al-Ṣamad." al-Ṣamad is a difficult word to translate. It means that God is eternal, absolute, independent, and completely depended upon by all else and at all moments. To use the words of the famous Qur'ān 'translator' Marmaduke Pickthall, God is "the eternally Besought of all!"[26] This highlights the availability of God at all moments of our existence, something which helped me realise I was able to call upon him whenever I wished to.

God then mentions explicitly what was suggested implicitly by the opening two sentences: Allah does not have children or parents. These familial links are traits of created beings; they are unsuitable for an independent God. God is without beginning and without end. He says elsewhere, "But His command, when He intends a thing, is only that He says unto it, 'Be!', and it is."[27] The Chapter of Sincerity then ends with God explaining that nothing is like Him. So much is explained in this chapter through 14 Arabic words. There is no book like the Qur᾽ān.

CHAPTER 5

THE PROBLEM OF EVIL

L ife is unpredictable. It may be running smoothly, with everything going your way, and then a tragedy occurs or something amazing happens and it changes the flow of your whole existence. Trials, tribulations, and hardships are a necessary part of life, no matter how much we try to shield ourselves from them. Natural disasters, such as earthquakes, tornadoes, droughts, and tsunamis, as well as man-made disasters, such as wars, pollution, and global warming, devastate lives across the globe. On a personal level, we all suffer both mentally and physically in different ways throughout our lives.

Atheists and those who believe in an impersonal God often reject religion because of the evil they see in the world. They ask how God could allow evil to exist when He could have just made everything good instead. This conundrum is famously called, 'The Problem of Evil'. David Hume wrote about God, "Is He willing to prevent evil, but not able? Then He is impotent. Is He able, but not willing? Then He is malevolent. Is He both able and willing? Whence then is evil?"[28]

This moral dilemma has led many people to atheism, including Ali Rizvi, who claims, in his book, "The Atheist Muslim," that the death of his 5-year-old cousin after a struggle with leukaemia is what led him to atheism.[29] He recalls standing at the bedside of his cousin confused and perplexed at what was going on. How was this suffering to be understood?

From an Islamic understanding, there is no problem of evil. One can understand how those in a secular world in which God—if He is even believed to exist—is seen as subservient and docile, working purely to bring about human pleasure and remove human suffering. This is not the Islamic understanding of God. Allah is The Merciful, He is The Mercifier, but He is also The Compeller, The Reckoner, The All-Powerful, and The All-Wise.

God is able to allow suffering, just as he is able to allow relief. In truth, there is no problem of evil, only a problem of arrogance. For people ask not what creates mischief but why upon God rests all judgement. They see something they dislike and consider its existence as evil. However, it may be the case that while what they see is evil, its existence is good and full of wisdom. God says, "Who has created life and death that He may try you [as to] which of you is best in conduct; and He is the Mighty, the Forgiving…"[30] Ali Rizvi's test was in front of him when he was stood at the bedside—was he going to abandon God at the site of suffering? He failed his test, but the door to forgiveness remains open.

Suffering is from the wisdom of God that he may or may not give us access to. It is not limited to humans, but is found across many creatures, each with their own purpose and aims. Further, God reassures us that accounts will be levelled in the Hereafter, a time when God will shower more mercy on humanity than He has done in this world. Fyodor Dostoevsky's character Ivan Fyodorovich laments in "The Brothers Karamazov" how no amount of good can justify hardship in the world.[31] This argument does not hold to logical or mathematical scrutiny.

If I were to ask anyone whether they were willing to take a small slap on the back of the hand for a thousand years of bliss, they would say, "Yes!" God is telling us that for finite hardship, however difficult it may seem, we may get infinite reward. Mathematically, if a large amount of bliss can overcome a small amount of hardship—and make it 'worth it'—then infinite bliss should be able to overcome any amount of hardship.

Further, there is no logical compulsion for such complaints. All of these arguments are purely emotional. They adhere to notions of good and evil and claim that evil should not exist because of whatever reasons. This is self-defeating. For the atheist, there is no good and evil—it is all just a mess of atoms without meaning. For the theist, it is God who is most knowledgeable, and God tells us He does things with wisdom and underlying mercy. In both of these scenarios, there can be no complaint. It is only if one takes an atheistic approach to religion and conflates the two, giving himself authority to demand actions from—and put limitations on—God that we arrive at this issue. There is a reason this issue does not affect truly spiritual men as much as it affects those who have secularised worldviews, even though the former are often the kindest, most charitable, and most empathetic people one comes across.

Our purpose in life is not to question God. God says, "He will not be questioned as to that which He doeth, but they will be questioned."[32] We expect trials and tribulations in life, enduring them through patience and submission to God, and expect, in return, His happiness and our eternal bliss. This is a trade most pleasing to those who possess both wisdom and humility.

Despite this, Islam does not encourage impotence. On the contrary, Muslims accept that the world is built on a system of cause and effect, and that part of our duty upon the earth is to relieve as much suffering as we can, and to bring about as much joy as we can. We act to the best of our ability, and that is a part of faith. The Prophet Muhammad [upon him be peace and blessings] once said, "Whoever among you sees an evil action and can change it with his hand [by taking action], let him change it with his hand. If he cannot do that, then with his tongue [by speaking out]. And if he cannot do that, then with his heart [by hating it and feeling that it is wrong]—and that is the weakest of faith."[33]

The true Muslim sees opportunity in every moment. The Prophet Muhammad [upon him be peace and blessings] said, "Strange are the ways of a believer, for there is good in every affair of his and this is not the case with anyone else except in the case of a believer, for if he has an occasion to feel delight, he thanks [God], thus there is a good for him in it, and if he gets into trouble and shows resignation [and endures it patiently], there is a good for him in it."[34] Like this, a believer traverses the earth in humble submission and wherever he sees evil, he works to correct it, and whenever he cannot correct it, he places his trust in God and resigns his affairs to Him.

During my years of suffering, I was facing challenges that seemed overwhelming, challenges that led to certain people before me committing suicide. Suicide was an option for me, too. My world seemed dark and hopeless at the time, and I had resorted to drink, drugs, and distraction before I complained to a God I did not believe in. Little did I know the felicity that path was leading to and the treasure I would soon find. Patience is difficult during hard times, but it is also mandatory that we exercise it to our utmost ability. We will not be brought to task for that which is beyond our capacity to control, but we are being tested in those matters we can control.

Two years ago, my father was diagnosed with Alzheimer's disease, a degenerative neurological condition for which we currently know no cure. I have seen my father deteriorate in front of my eyes. Initially, he would forget simple things like his keys or glasses. Now, he sometimes forgets who I am and who his wife is. He can barely walk, and he struggles with frequent delusions. My mother has her own health conditions to contend with. My father's mental health is a real test for my mother and I, and it is one in which we need to show patience.

Throughout all of our lives, we reach situations which cause us to be distressed. We may be perplexed and unable to make sense of what is happening. There have been plenty of times in my own life in which I wished I could just run away from my problems. It took a while for me to learn that running away is neither a solution for the problem at hand nor a fulfilment of my purpose in life. Instead of trying to escape life's challenges, we should tackle them and work towards a better world. Whatever evil we fail to overcome despite our best efforts, we dislike in our hearts and then we resign the matter to God.

In the Qur'ān, we find an encapsulating tale about the Prophet Moses [upon him be peace] and a man known as al-Khiḍr [upon him be peace], about whom little is known. The story discusses a time when Moses and those with him met al-Khiḍr, God says, "Then they found a slave from among Our slaves unto whom We had given mercy from Us and had taught knowledge from Our presence."

Moses asked al-Khiḍr whether he may accompany him, saying, "May I follow you so that you may teach me from what you have been taught of sound judgement?"[35] al-Khiḍr responded, "Truly, you will not be able to bear with me patiently. And how could you be patient in matters beyond your knowledge?"[36] al-Khiḍr seemed to know something that Moses did not. Moses was aware of this, but he was not aware of just how difficult it can be to accept that which one cannot understand fully.

Moses is famed for his sense of justice and willingness to exert himself, despite the costs, in his pursuit of goodness. In many ways, al-Khiḍr can be seen to represent qadr [destiny] incarnate. al-Khiḍr agreed to travel with Moses on condition that the latter does not lose his patience. He asked of Moses, "If you follow me, then do not query anything I do before I mention it to you myself."[37] Moses knew from God that al-Khiḍr was a good man, and that he was someone who had been given knowledge that was not given to Moses, so he agreed and followed him.

The story moves captivatingly through a series of curious occurrences:

> "Moses said, 'God willing, you will find me patient. I will not disobey you in any way.' The man said, 'If you follow me then, do not query anything I do before I mention it to you myself.' They travelled on. Later, when they got into a boat, and the man made a hole in it, Moses said, 'How could you make a hole in it? Do you want to drown its passengers? What a strange thing to do!' He replied, 'Did I not tell you that you would never be able to bear with me patiently?' Moses said, 'Forgive me for forgetting. Do not make it too hard for me to follow you.' And so they travelled on. Then, when they met a young boy and the man killed him, Moses said, 'How could you kill an innocent person? He has not killed anyone! What a terrible thing to do!' He replied, 'Did I not tell you that you would never be able to bear with me patiently?' Moses said, 'From now on, if I query anything you do, banish me from your company—you have put up with enough from me.' And so they travelled on. Then, when they came to a town and asked the inhabitants for food but were refused hospitality, they saw a wall there that was on the point of falling down and the man repaired it. Moses said, 'But if you had wished you could have taken payment for do-

ing that.' He said, 'This is where you and I part company. I will tell you the meaning of the things you could not bear with patiently: as for the ship, it belonged to poor people working at sea. So I intended to cause a defect in it as there was after them a king who seized every [good] ship by force. And as for the boy, his parents were believers, and we feared that he would overburden them by transgression and disbelief. So we intended that their Lord should substitute for them one better than him in purity and nearer to mercy. As for the wall, it belonged to two young orphans in the town and there was buried treasure beneath it belonging to them. Their father had been a righteous man, so your Lord intended them to reach maturity and then dig up their treasure as a mercy from your Lord. I did not do [these things] of my own accord: these are the explanations for those things you could not bear with patience.'"[38]

On each occasion, Moses' sense of justice led him to want to change the course of events, however, al-Khiḍr was aware of something deeper at work. In no way are we allowed to imitate the actions of al-Khiḍr ourselves—we are not prophets and we must act according to what we are capable of. Similarly, Moses was responding in a way that was natural to him given the knowledge he had and that he was a wise, God-fearing, and patient man, but his sense of justice led to repeated interjections, which then led al-Khiḍr to part from his company. If even Moses was not aware of all the world's wisdoms, then how could we expect to be so?

Our task in life is to do as much good as we can, and to prevent as much evil as we can. We all hate to see the suffering of innocents, and we should work diligently to relieve this suffering through whatever means are available to us. As for those problems beyond our control, we pray to God to help those in need. As for those He does not help materially in the world, we expect that they will receive perfect justice in the world to come.

This book of mine, which I pen know with an open heart, is one of the benefits behind the suffering I endured for so many years. I hope others lower their guard and see the light as I have seen it. I am reminded of a quote I once heard and cannot now reference, though it stuck with me, "In every calamity there is a scholarship to be gained which can only be gained by those who show patience."

CHAPTER 6

SPEAKERS' CORNER

Da'wah, in Arabic, means 'making an invitation'. Used unqualifiedly, it often refers to inviting people to Islam. Scrolling through YouTube, I came across a number of da'wah videos. It was these that began my journey into the field of da'wah. At the time, I didn't even know what the word meant. Arabic words are typically based on trilateral or quadrilateral roots that are composed of consonants and give meanings to the variations that stem from them. The trilateral root of da'wah is: dā, 'ayn, and waw. This root gives a meaning of support, strength, reinforcement, and consolidation. It was this strength that I wished to give to my fellow humans.

Throughout my time scrolling through YouTube, I came across myriad weird and wonderful videos, as well as many anti-Islam videos. I then clicked on a set of da'wah videos by Hamza Tzortzis, a man I now consider a dear friend. At the time, I was unaware of who he was. What I did know, however, is that he presented Islam and its intellectual foundations in an honest, open, and powerful way. I was captivated.

Until this point, my journey into Islam had been through intuition, basic reasoning, and my own life journey. I had not formally studied Islam or philosophy, and I was unaware of so many of the intellectual roots that Hamza discussed. Using the arguments he presented, I engaged in discussions with family, friends, acquaintances, and even strangers online. I just wanted to share the beautiful message I had received.

After asking God to guide me and show me the way, I came upon a da'wah course which was to be hosted by Hamza Tzortzis himself—I immediately signed up. The course was so much more than I could have reasonably expected. Hamza was affable and there were so many people from different walks of life who gathered with a shared aim. The polemics I had learned previously were honed and Hamza kindly gave me some direction going forward. I asked God to allow me to work within the field of da'wah, not knowing how soon this prayer would be answered.

A few years later, I would return to this same course at the same university it was initially hosted at. This time, however, I would be hosting the course. My prayer was eventually answered, even if it took me a while to get to that stage. Prior to that, I had begun to feel dissatisfied with my da'wah output considering how much I had learned. There wasn't much that I was doing, and this fact was starting to irritate me.

My 9-5 job of working as a designer in London did not bring me a sense of fulfilment and accomplishment. What I really wanted to do was to share the message of Islam with as many people as I could. Not doing so weighed heavily on my heart. My place of employment had a rooftop terrace from which you could see the City of London skyline. It was a place I would go for lunch and some fresh air, a welcome break from the office. I would always eat my lunch there, and I would even pray my morning prayers there.

As I finished my lunch, my phone rang. It was from an unknown number—usually I decline these calls—but I answered the call. It was an employee from iERA, a company that Hamza Tzortzis was a part of. We exchanged pleasantries, and then he asked whether I had been involved in any da'wah work since I had attended the course. Guiltily, I replied in the negative. He responded saying there was a local da'wah team in West Ealing that regularly ran a da'wah stall. He asked whether I would be interested in joining them. "Yes!" I responded unthinkingly.

For the next year and a half, I was a regular at the West Ealing da'wah stall, engaging with all those willing to come and talk. There appeared to be a lot of misconceptions about Islam among the public, but also an earnestness and willingness to learn more when things were presented to them honestly and openly. Quickly, these misconceptions would topple and people would begin to discuss the deeper questions in life.

It wasn't long before I discovered Speakers' Corner, London's infamous public venue for unofficial debates and speeches. It is located in Hyde Park and topics of discussion include religion, philosophy, and politics. Around a decade ago, when I would frequent Speakers' Corner, it was quite different to how it is now. Back then, there were less cameras around and debates were less theatrical and more honest. Discussions were largely meaningful.

During my initial few visits, I went as a spectator, observing the discussions and those listening. It appeared that most people who came in search for answers were only really willing to listen to those who shared their views. This phenomenon is common in our culture, and it leads to huge echo chambers in real life or online.

Eventually, I began engaging in discussions at Speaker's Corner myself, learning quickly that I was somewhat of a natural orator. People seemed to enjoy the way I spoke and I grew in confidence myself. Soon, I began to climb the ladder at Speakers' Corner every week to address the crowd. The few cameras that were present began to record my speeches and upload them to YouTube along with some of my discussions with atheists.

Subboor Ahmed was a close friend of mine from iERA and we decided to start our own YouTube channel where we could upload our talks and discussions from Speaker's Corner. We realised that doing so allowed us to reach a much wider audience than we did in Hyde Park alone. As the years past, my popularity among the Muslim public grew, and I was regularly invited to give talks at universities and mosques from across the globe.

In 2013, I received an offer to officially work for iERA. This was a dream opportunity for me. It would allow me to focus full-time on da'wah and work alongside Hamza Tzortzis himself, who was one of iERA's leading outreach specialists at the time. I pounced upon the offer.

My life was changing rapidly. Over the space of a few years, I had moved from being a tormented and lost soul without a known purpose to a man who was healed and out to heal others. The more I studied, the more my faith grew and the more popular I became. This popularity meant I was incredibly busy, leaving little time to focus on myself. One risks losing themselves physically and spiritually if they are not careful. Being busy can lead to sloth and being popular can lead to arrogance. I needed to be on the lookout for both.

Studying hard meant I quickly sifted through all the major arguments for and against the existence of God. I studied philosophy, including the philosophy of science. I studied the new '-isms' of the age and the New Atheist movement. It was vital that I remained aware of the ideologies affecting the hearts and minds of the people of our time. Repeatedly during my studies, I was awestruck at the beauty of Islam and the strength of its intellectual foundations. I remember being speechless when I first came across Hamza Tzortzis' Qurʾanic argument for God—how beautifully he uprooted every alternative until the only possibility that remained was the existence of God.

"This Qurʾān could only be the word of God," I remember thinking, as I read the following from the Qurʾān, "Or were they created out of naught? Or are they the creators? Or did they create the heavens and the earth? Nay, but they are sure of nothing!"[39] Three rhetorical questions were asked:

i.   Did man arise spontaneously from nothingness?

ii. Did man create himself?

iii. Did man create the universe?

As for the first question, it was clear that nothingness gives rise to nothing. Saying that something arose from 'nothing' is treating this 'nothing' as a thing. People often imagine nothingness as empty space, but this is completely not the case. Empty space is still a physical space, which is a thing. The best definition of 'nothing' that I have come across is that it is "that which rocks dream of." Rocks do not dream, and if anybody were to even suggest that the dream of a rock led to the existence of a universe, they would be assessed for insanity. It belies logic.

As for the second question, it highlights how people circularly reason to delude themselves. Man cannot possibly create himself as, to do so, he would have had to exist—in order to carry out the act of creating himself—prior to his existence. The incoherence of this claim is clear.

As for the third question, the obvious answer is "No. Man is thoroughly incapable of creating the whole universe, with its complexity, size, and power." However, this question leads to another, "Could any created thing theoretically lead to the creation of a universe?" This proposal includes theories such as the multiverse theory. Were we to accept that a universe could create another—something for which we have no evidence—it would still not solve the issue. What would result is an infinite chain of universes going back in time. This would mean an infinite amount of time spent creating universes would be needed to reach our present moment in creation, and an infinite can definitionally never be traversed. Thus, the infinite regress that results is a logical impossibility. Further, an infinite regress fails to answer the two questions of how things are the way they are and why things are the way they are. These infinite regresses are the bane of atheist polemicists the world over.

Using a less abstract example, we can consider the situation of a man who wishes to ride a bus. He needs £1 to do so, but he has no money on him. He turns around and asks the man behind him for £1. The man replies he does not have £1 and then proceeds to turn around and ask the man behind him. This third man says he does not have £1 and then proceeds to turn around and ask the man behind him. This cycle continues infinitely. Will the first man ever receive £1? The answer is clearly no. Only if someone breaks the chain and offers £1 will the first man ever receive £1.

All this was understood when I read those sentences from the Qur'ān. Every time I recited them in my mind, I would come to the conclusion that God necessarily exists. Those rhetorical questions made me think about the world, and each time I did, my belief in God increased palpably.

CHAPTER 7

YET ANOTHER WAVE

Being engrossed in da'wah meant that I neglected myself. Things had slowly been changing over time and I was not being mindful of my intention and sincerity. My intention began to drift from pleasing God to pleasing the people. This is clear in retrospect but, at the time, I struggled to realise.

Before this period, my life was unfulfilled, and suddenly, it became difficult not to overindulge. For me, the indulgences began with smaller thing, like zealously checking how many views my videos were getting—the popularity was intoxicating. People's praise began to feel good and I would try to convince myself that I didn't care for their praise. I would put a positive spin on each moment of vanity, convincing myself that more views meant more people would benefit, and so I shouldn't be ashamed of my lusting over my view counts.

Without realising, I was falling into the same trap from which I had escaped—I was becoming enslaved to the opinions and whims of others. My happiness was becoming dependent on the approval of my audience and peers. The beauty that I had found in detaching myself from this enslavement and submitting, instead, to my Lord was vanishing. This was another test for me. Growing up, during my bouts of existential angst, I felt that I did not fit in with the popular and carefree children around me. All this approval appeared to me now like a feast appears to a starved man.

As my love for fame and recognition grew, my desire to connect with God shrunk. My prayers were becoming less timely and less solemn. I never stopped praying the five daily prayers, but my prayers themselves were turning into purely mechanistic actions. In the field of da'wah, this is a potentially fatal misstep as one's work requires great spiritual resolve and a strong connection with God.

My spiritual heart was dying and I was ignoring the warning signs that came my way, telling myself that it was only a small issue and convincing myself that I was stronger than I really was. My ego was being fed constantly—each 'win' in an argument attested to my greatness, or so I thought. This is not how da'wah is meant to be done.

Abū Ḥanīfa [upon him be mercy], a famous early Muslim jurist, once advised his son Ḥammād [upon him be mercy] to stop debating theology. Ḥammād responded that he remembered seeing Abū Ḥanīfa himself debate people. Abū Ḥanīfa replied, "We debated and it was as if birds were sat atop our heads [i.e. we were humble and nervous], lest our opponent slipped [and said something evil]." True da'wah is not about looking good in an argument, it is about behaving and calling in the best of manners, so that those who come across you are emotionally and intellectually inclined to see the light.

My behaviour was not without consequence. Once again in my life, the world became dark. I remember, vividly, resting in my house and feeling a heaviness in my chest. The sensation grew and panic began to creep in as I lay there still. Frantically, I glanced around the room, unsure of what was going on. My emotions were suddenly dulling and I heard a strange humming sound in my ears. The emptiness was returning—it felt almost visceral.

All of this happened so suddenly that I barely had time to make sense of it. I had somehow left the state of bliss I was in and returned to the dread from which I had escaped. The cause of my distress seems obvious with hindsight, as do most things, but at the time, I was bewildered and in denial. It was difficult to accept that I was having a spiritual crisis when I was not only aware of the truth but was sharing it with others.

The responsibility of sharing Islam with others, coupled with the hypocrisy I felt from my arrogant behaviour, was incredibly burdensome. Living through this contradiction was difficult and I was about to quit the da'wah until I had rectified my soul internally. On further introspection, I thought that leaving the da'wah could be fatal for my soul, as the company I now kept offered me a thread of hope and revival.

It wasn't clear to me why I felt like this internally when nothing had changed intellectually. I remember teaching people about da'wah and how to call to God's way when I, myself, had lost my way. It wasn't easy. My struggles were likely showing in my demeanour. This dichotomous life went on for months. I would go to the mosque and cry in silence at my state, hoping to find relief. I tried to prostrate in the same way I had done years earlier before being unshackled from my mental anguish. With my head upon the ground I begged, "O God, please help me out of this situation. Please remove this state from me. I understand my fault. I forgot You and remembered others." This time, however, I felt nothing after the prostration.

One evening in the mosque, immediately after the evening prayer, I sat and reflected over everything that had happened. Broken-hearted, and with my eyes closed, I spoke in silence to God. I knew how distant I had become and how much I had abused the favours bestowed upon me. Without words, I expressed my brokenness and exhaustion to God. As I was sat contemplating, I felt a consoling hand land upon my shoulder. I opened my eyes to see who this was and there was no one there. This was a sign from the One who hears prayers. God says, "And when My servants question you concerning Me, then surely I am near. I answer the prayer of the supplicant when he cries unto Me. So let them hear My call and let them trust in Me in order that they may be led aright."[40]

Needing time to work on myself and feeling unable to continue living a dual existence, I left social media and stepped back from hosting da'wah courses and delivering lectures. I needed time to work on myself.

With time to myself now, I set out to systematically identify what was distressing me. I revisited every rational proof of God I knew, checking to see whether anything had changed. Every argument was just as logically coherent as it had been before, and all of it made complete sense. For example, the 'Kalām Cosmological' argument was a powerful one for me when I was learning about God initially and it remained just as powerful now. Retracing the logical steps affirmed how watertight these arguments are to a reasonable mind.

Looking back over my notes, Hamza Tzortzis' academic output, and myriad sources, my intellectual faith was reaffirmed. William Lane Craig, adapting al-Ghazālī's [upon him be mercy] argument, posits the following:

P1: Everything that begins to exist has a cause of its existence.

P2: The universe began to exist.

P3: Therefore, the universe has a cause of its existence.

P4: No scientific explanation using physics, biology, or chemistry can provide a causal account of the origin of the universe, as these are a part of the universe itself.

C1: Therefore, the cause of the universe must be personal.[41]

Craig went on to explain how God is the only possible 'personal' creator of the universe. al-Ghazālī used concepts such as the absurdity of infinite regresses of temporal events to evidence his positions. I delved into how each proposition above was defended and how the conclusions were reached. I also studied, again, so many other arguments for God, reading the counterarguments of atheists and the contentions of those who chose to disbelieve. All of this strengthened my intellectual faith even more. It was clear that God exists.

So why was I so upset? Upon reflection, I began to realise that one can be rationally convinced of God yet remain distant from Him, cut off from experience the sweetness of faith. Conversely, one may experience faith without any rational proofs, just as one experiences mind, thought, and existence without rational argumentation. This is how I felt when I first embraced Islam—I tasted it, to borrow the language of the mystics. Now, I had found myself on the opposite side of the spectrum, a rational believer who was missing the beauty of faith. God says, "Have these people not travelled through the land with hearts to understand and ears to hear? It is not people's eyes that are blind, but their hearts within their breasts."[42]

This was my state—I had closed my spiritual heart to faith whilst accepting it rationally and opposing it through my arrogance and conceit. Through feeding my ego I was starving my heart, and as I lived in opposition to my beliefs, I became agitated internally. Many people have experienced similar states. The 'solution' is either to realign one's actions with their beliefs or to let go of those beliefs entirely. A hypocritical life is not an option if one wishes to be at peace.

The easiest of these two solutions is often to let go of one's beliefs, as this typically requires no changes in one's lifestyle. To facilitate this, we often begin to create false narratives that justify our actions. We begin to doubt the truth without logical reasons. We look for ways to make the truth seem unappealing in an effort to remove our guilt for abandoning it.

Through my time in the field of da'wah, I came across many people who had fallen into the above trap. Before finding answers to one's doubts, I would first try to identify why their doubts arose in the first place. In the overwhelming majority of cases, the reason was that the person wished to do something which God had forbidden. This would then lead to an internal struggle, and the person's faith would grow weak. The person would then be open to accept any number of doubts—no matter how flimsy—and take them as valid reasons to abandon faith.

They would have done well to pay attention to God's words where He said, "Say, 'O My servants who have transgressed against themselves [by sinning], do not despair of the mercy of Allah. Indeed Allah forgives all sins. Indeed, it is He who is the Forgiving, the Merciful.'"[43] Man is a weak creature, often falling prey to whim and vice. I, myself, indulged in vanity and arrogance, preferring fame to the pleasure of God, and this was nearly fatal. God does not accept partners in love and deeds—that is to say that He does not accept that we love anyone as we should love Him and He does not accept any act of worship [including da'wah] that is done for both Him and another being. The result of my misdeeds was that my heart felt distant from God and my mind was afflicted by doubts, even though it was rationally convinced of the truth of Islam.

God's mercy is vast and, as a result, He gives people multiple chances. He gave me an opportunity to repent, learn, and grow. This second crisis of faith led me to the realisation that faith is not dependent on rational argumentation. Faith is something given by God to the believers. Rational proofs work to strengthen one's faith and to rekindle the natural disposition that inheres within every human and yearns for God, but without the favour of God, one can never reach Him.

In Islam, this innate disposition of man is known as the fiṭrah. The word 'fiṭrah' has the trilateral root of fā, ṭā, and rā, which gives meanings of: making, creating, bringing into being, bringing forth, endowing, passing, being naturally disposed to, being innately characterised by, and so on. The fiṭrah of man yearns to worship God. Many studies have now demonstrated this fact, including a recent study with 57 researchers and a budget of £1,900,000 conducted by the University of Oxford which demonstrated this phenomenon even in children younger than five years of age.[44] As we grow and the distractions of the world are presented to us, we can forget this part of ourselves, and once forgotten, it can prove extremely difficult to find again.

CHAPTER 8

THE FACULTIES OF MAN

My wounds had scarcely begun healing from the trauma of this internal crisis before another one came. My father suddenly became ill and was hospitalised as a result. During his inpatient stay, he contracted a gastrointestinal illness which exacerbated his situation and meant he wouldn't leave hospital for several days at least. He had been suffering from memory loss and the early stages of Alzheimer's disease, both of which predispose one to becoming delirious in a new setting, such as a hospital. This is what happened to my father.

My father was unable to recognise me—something which caused me excruciating pain—and he would wake up confused in the middle of the night, unaware of where he was and how he got there. We were soon released home and told that delirium often resolves when a patient returns to more familiar surroundings. At the time, I was not aware that this visit would be the first of several hospital admissions in the coming months.

When visiting my dad, I would sit beside him as he rested. On the opposite side of the ward was another elderly man who was often visited by his wife. This man would fall asleep and his wife would remain sat by his side. He would wake up every couple of minutes and glance around the room, confused and unaware of where he was. His wife would remind him each time that he was in the hospital. On one occasion, this cycle repeated itself for a whole hour.

It struck me that the man's actions were a metaphor for many of our lives. He had all the physical faculties necessary to identify his whereabouts, but he was failing to make the relevant links and was lost in confusion. We have all been given the tools to discern the truth from falsehood yet so many of us fail to use them appropriately.

Taking the example of the natural sciences; our ability to engage in them is a miracle. There is a teleological proof to be found in the 'laws' of physics if one reflects deeply. Nothing logically compels randomness to produce such consistent laws, yet the consistency in these laws and their precision means we can calculate, predict, and study the material world in all its majesty. The fact that we have order instead of chaos is itself a miracle. Were the world truly a chaotic jumble of matter, then the law of entropy would prohibit the existence of any order. Despite this, instead of being awestruck and falling prostrate in gratitude for the Creator of these laws, many people unthinkingly deem the laws to be self-sustaining truths. They are unable to see past the material world.

Even our ability to reason and manipulate abstract information is a miracle. That we have a mind beyond physical processes and an identity we are aware of is a miracle. We are sentient and have consciousness. These faculties have been given to us for a reason—our ultimate purpose is to worship God. God says, "And Allah has extracted you from the wombs of your mothers not knowing a thing, and He made for you hearing and vision and hearts [i.e., intellect] that perhaps you would be grateful."[45]

Sadly, much of humanity has taken these faculties and rebelled against the One who gave them to them. Science is somehow seen as a replacement for religion. This is nonsensical. Religious theists—

Muslims, even—invented the scientific method. Science explores the natural world and helps us gain some control over it, but much to the displeasure of people like Richard Dawkins, science is not able to answer the big questions in life. It has never been able to and will never be able to answer everything, as demonstrated by Gödel in his famous incompleteness theorem.[46]

Historically, scientists were aware of the distinction between what could be studied through the scientific method and what could not. Descartes famously divided existence into body and mind—dualism. He then aimed to study the body in a purely mechanistic manner, avoiding resorting to any mystical forces. Descartes wished to describe the world through a system of pulleys and levers, and he had some success.[47] Cartesian mechanism began gaining traction across Europe. Much to the dismay of his followers, however, Isaac Newton, who came only 46 years later, firmly reintroduced mystical forces in the world with his theory of gravity. Two objects being able to attract without ever touching is impossible in a system of pulleys and levers. Nor is it possible in any mechanistic understanding of the world, including Einstein's theories of space-time. All problems like these—without exception—remain unexplained and unexplainable through purely naturalistic worldviews.

To quote Dr Allan Chapman, an established professor based at The University of Oxford, and regular visiting professor to Gresham College, "After its first publication in 1687, there were two further editions of Principia in Newton's lifetime, in 1713 and 1726, the latter only a few months before his death. The later editions contained ideas and information not present in the first. One very important idea concerned the very nature of gravity itself. For Cartesian physicists in continental Europe had criticised Newton for bringing occult, mystical, and invisible forces back into physics which Descartes' swirling vortices had supposedly banished, and which it had been one of the key purposes of Book II to refute. But towards the end of the 1713 edition, in the newly added concluding 'General Scholium' essay, Newton came to grips with some of the more philosophical implications of his gravitation theory. He plainly admitted that he had no idea what gravity was as a physical entity; what he was doing was elucidating the exact mathematical laws in accordance with which gravity acted. As Newton phrased it in the Latin, hypotheses non fingo, or 'I frame no hypotheses' about what gravity is. Gravity simply exists and acts. There is evidence that Newton, who was deeply learned theologically as well as mathematically, saw gravity as an aspect of God's power, the action of which the Almighty had revealed to the human intellect through mathematics. But that was all. As a concept, however, Newton's recognition of the ultimate un-knowableness of the nature of gravity was to have an immensely liberating effect upon subsequent science, as future generations of scientists no longer saw themselves as having to explain the powers of nature [such as light, electromagnetism, or by the 1840s, energy itself], but rather as free to explore their physical properties and to establish exact mathematical expressions for the same. For it came to be accepted that it was the scientist's job to describe nature and to elucidate nature's laws, and that it was the task of the theologian or the philosopher to explore why these laws were so."[48]

Scientists went on to do just that, describe the world of matter. Noam Chomsky laments at how atheists of today like to gloss over this history and reality, pretending, instead, that their natural science truly addresses the big questions.[49] The truth is far from this. As Allan Chapman mentioned above, scientists gave up on addressing problems such as the hard problem of consciousness and atheists tried to pretend these problems don't exist. Thankfully, the world is changing again and people are realising how untenable these positions are. Science and religion complement each other and, when combined, lead to a much more holistic and true-to-life understanding of the world.

Back at home, my father's illness had progressed to the point that he was unable to carry out activities of daily living. He was unable to dress and wash, wholly dependent on support from his family members. Meanwhile, my daughter was 3 years old by now and was becoming increasingly independent as time went on. Life is a cycle and we should be grateful for our health and mental capabilities before they eventually leave us. God says, "Allah is He who shaped you out of weakness, then appointed after weakness strength, then, after strength, appointed weakness and grey hair. He creates what He will. He is the Knower, the Mighty."[50]

Despite my father's mental deterioration, he remained a firm believer in God. He would remember God even when he would have bouts of delirium and lose familiarity with his environment and close family members. The reality of God seemed a more pre-eminent truth in his mind than the specifics of the world. Perhaps this was because his faith stemmed from something subconscious: his fiṭrah [innate natural predisposition].

I noticed a similar phenomenon in my daughter. She was beginning to exhibit signs of this fiṭrī compulsion towards God. She would make causal links between phenomena and relate events back to the will of God. Whenever we spoke about God, she would acknowledge what I said as if it was something she already understood, at least in part. She was not like this with regards to the rest of the world—in other discussions, she was headstrong and opinionated. Convincing her to eat dinner, watch less cartoons, or go to bed on time was a real challenge. It was only in theological discussions that she demonstrates such a beautiful affinity. She innately understood God and our relationship to him.

I mentioned earlier how this affinity is demonstrable through studies, and here we have an anecdotal case study. What makes a per son leave this predisposition and reject God as they grow is never the result of objective thought. Societal pressures, a willingness to do that which religion forbids, emotional states, and a false sense of independence are typically at play behind such a rejection. The unbeliever may return to what his innermost self was calling him to, or he may drown this innermost self in the distractions of the world.

Often, it is at times of difficulty and hardship that a person snaps out of the hypnotic allure of the world and returns to God. This reminds me of the story of a friend of mine that he once relayed to me. My friend went to visit some of his friends and they all sat together watching TV in a living room. Meanwhile one of their sons was outside in the street playing. Suddenly, they heard tyres screeching followed by a loud bang. The child's mother jumped out of her chair and repeatedly screamed, "O my God! O my God!" as she went in search of her child. She returned moments later with her child safely in her arms, exclaiming, "Thank God! Thank God! Thank God!" There was widespread relief that the child was unharmed.

After the dust had settled, my friend couldn't help but reflect over the mother's reaction. She was an atheist but, upon the mere thought of a calamity, she immediately resorted to calling out to God. It was instant and intuitive. He thought it must have been her fiṭrah speaking and so he asked her, "Marie, if you don't mind me asking, why did you call out to God when you were alarmed and then why did you thank him when you found your child safe?" She responded defensively, saying, "It is just a figure of speech." "I appreciate that, but that's not how you usually respond when things go wrong. You normally shout through a list of expletives," my friend averred. Marie began to reflect over what he was saying and she muttered, "That's true... I don't know why I said that." My friend then proddingly asked, "Could it be that the gravity of the situation—as your child meant more to you than even your own life—meant that you lowered your guard and acknowledged something you believe deep down as you hoped that God would save him?" Marie thought for a while in silence and then responded, "I don't know."

During moments such as these, in which we find ourselves broken, we become forced to acknowledge our own weakness and we become humble. At these moments, our ego lowers and we are more able to accept the truths we are innately predisposed to accepting. Edgar Harrell, one of the 300 survivors of the sinking USS Indianapolis—the last ship to be sunk by enemy contact in the Second World War—once wrote, "You see maybe a body on an eight-foot swell. And all of the sudden that swell breaks and that body comes down and he hits you and he leaves that residue on you. And you see that and say, "Is that going to be me tomorrow or yet today?". And see you look up. And may I say, 'There is no such thing as atheists in foxholes. There were no atheists out there'... Everyone prayed. I can hear one of those sailors praying today, 'God if you are out there. I don't want to die. I have a son back home that I have never seen. I want to live, but we have to have help.' So we prayed and we prayed and we continued to pray."[51]

Edgar's son, David Harrell, would later write in a book about his father, "Clearly there were no atheists in the water that day. Gone was that damnable attitude of pride that deceives men into thinking that there is no God, or if there is, they don't need Him. When a man is confronted with death, it is the face of Almighty God he sees, not his own. We were all acutely aware of our Creator during those days and nights."[52]

Eva Hart, a British woman who survived the sinking of the Titanic, reported that when her mother asked a crewmember about the ensuing drama aboard the ship, the response came that, "God himself could not sink this ship."[53] How wrong this response proved to be.

As the ship began to sink, the band reportedly played music to calm the panic but some passengers requested that hymns be played instead.

Steve Turner, author of "The Band That Played On: The Extraordinary Story of the 8 Musicians Who Went Down with the Titanic," reports that Carlos Hurd jotted down many eyewitness accounts from another ship out at sea that night, writing, "As the screams in the water multiplied, another sound was heard, strong and clear at first, then fainter in the distance. It was the melody of the hymn 'Nearer, My God, to Thee,' played by the string orchestra in the dining saloon. Some of those on the water started to sing the words..."[54]

This fiṭrī yearning for God in one's final moments is attested to throughout history and across the land and sea. The Qur'ān spoke of this phenomenon, making specific reference to case of ships out at sea. God says, "[Prophet], do you not see that ships sail through the sea, by the grace of God, to show you [people] some of His wonders? Truly there are signs in this for every steadfast, thankful person. When the waves loom over those on board like giant shadows they call out to God, devoting their religion entirely to Him. But, when He has delivered them safely to land, some of them waver—only a treacherous, thankless person refuses to acknowledge Our signs."[55]

Studying the fiṭrah allowed me to connect a lot of the dots in my own life. Why I behaved the way I did and why I felt the way I did when I stopped focusing on my relationship with God. It was my fiṭrah that initially brought me to Islam. Rational proofs further convinced me and strengthened my intellectual faith, but Islam is not like the natural sciences, it necessitates that one drops his ego and submits himself to God alone.

CHAPTER 9
RAḤMA/MERCY

After one faces a frightening storm, he becomes alert and acutely aware of the unpredictability of life. He realises how little control he truly has over his life and his façade of independence falls down. Many of us are deluded and think that relying upon God means abandoning the physical means to achieve a purpose. This is not what Islam teaches.

Even Mary [upon her be peace], mother of Jesus [upon him be peace], needed to exert herself to receive sustenance during labour. God says, "And so it was ordained: she conceived him. She withdrew to a distant place and, when the pains of childbirth drove her to [cling to] the trunk of a palm tree, she exclaimed, 'I wish I had been dead and forgotten long before all this!' but a voice cried to her from below, 'Do not worry: your Lord has provided a stream at your feet and, if you shake the trunk of the palm tree towards you, it will deliver fresh ripe dates for you, so eat, drink, be glad, and say to anyone you may see, 'I have vowed to the Lord of Mercy to abstain from conversation, and I will not talk to anyone today.'"[56]

Mary was going through intense hardship and God could have granted her sustenance without her even needing to move, but He tasked her with shaking the trunk of the palm tree—she was tasked with an action that was within her capabilities and God took care of the rest. Earlier in her life, Mary would receive food directly from

God, prepared and ready at her place of worship. It was a miracle given to this blessed woman. At times in life, we may also receive favours we did not work for, but that should not stop us working towards that which we are capable of working towards.

Managing my condition and my father's illness was very difficult for me. I understood that behind all of this was wisdom. Climbing out of the mountain of hardship looked difficult, but it was something I needed to do—I needed to act. Little did I know, the journey was about to be made much harder. On a wintry December night, my wife attended a routine check-up appointment for her pregnancy. Her blood pressure was worryingly high, and after deliberating, her doctor informed us that she was suffering from pre-eclampsia, a potentially life-threatening complication of pregnancy.

The doctors decided to induce labour two weeks early due to the risks of not doing so being so great. The induction failed and, after 48 hours, her blood pressure remained dangerously high. We were told the safest course of action at that moment was to undergo an emergency c-section. I remember the adrenaline rushing through my veins as the doctors discussed the c-section. I remember having to sign the consent form on behalf of my wife as she was too exhausted to comprehend what was going on. I remember being helpless as I sat beside her whilst the doctors operated.

I remember hearing a cry—my daughter was born.

It is difficult to put into words what that moment felt like. Becoming a parent is a surreal moment shared by so many of us. At that moment, I experienced a rush of happiness and relief. A new person had entered my life and I loved her dearly. Looking into her large eyes for the first time, I felt I already knew her. It was both strange and beautiful.

In the background, I heard the surgeon say with a worried tone, "She's losing a lot of blood!" Panic ensued. I stared at the surgeons and cried out, "What's going on?" My heart was in my mouth. They informed me that my wife's womb was not contracting as it normally should and that she was losing a lot of blood as a result. They told me not to worry but they looked so obviously worried themselves.

The situation was tense and neither I nor the surgeons knew what the outcome would be. Immediately, my thoughts rushed towards God, and in a moment in which I truly appreciated by own helplessness, I called upon God, "Please save her! Only You can save her! No one has any true power except You! Please save her!"

A few attempts to remedy the issue by the surgeons failed, but then suddenly, they managed to usher the womb to contract and stem the flow of blood. My prayer had been answered. As I mentioned earlier, we carry out whatever actions we are able to and leave the rest to God. Like when Mary [upon her be peace] shook the palm tree, we do our best through whatever means are available to us, but God decides the ultimate outcome. This was something made crystal clear to me on that day. Never before had I understood this concept so well. It took me feeling utterly hopeless and then completely rescued—whilst seeing surgeons use all at their means to help my wife and I—before I appreciated how God had fashioned this world of cause and effect, a world that was always ultimately dependent on Him.

My wife was saved and my attention returned to my daughter. She was tiny, weighing no more than five pounds at birth. It was incredibly surreal to think that a few moments ago she did not exist in the world, and that now she was a small baby in the big wide world and soon she will be a walking, talking child, and then she will be an adult, making her own impact on our world. Life itself is a sign of

God. God says, "He created man from a drop of fluid, and yet man openly challenges Him."

My gratitude was tinged with the remorse I felt for having distanced myself from God over the past months. This remorse made me feel even more grateful—despite my shortcomings, I was still blessed. I realised then that we can never be grateful enough. God's infinite mercy is beyond our limited gratitude, and his ultimate justice is above our chequered emotions.

We named our daughter Aisha. She brought with her myriad blessings. My father quickly recovered from the acute stage of his illness and my wife was also making a swift recovery. As things were normalising, my focus returned to my own soul. The recent events had done well to rectify many of my problems, but I still had some way to go on my journey.

Kintsugi is the Japanese art of fixing broken pieces of pottery using gold. The idea is to make the new piece more beautiful than the first. Not only have you remedied an issue, but you have reached something more beautiful in the process. Life is also sometimes like that. Your life breaks down, only for you to work through the challenges, face your demons, and emerge as a better and more rounded person than you were before. Each time I focused on improving my relationship with God, my chest expanded and my anxiety calmed. Little-by-little, I was healing.

CHAPTER 10

MAKKAH

On a cold winter morning, I was heading to Gatwick airport to catch a flight to Jeddah, Saudi Arabia via Istanbul, Turkey. I arrived at the airport early and had a few hours to while away. My friend Awais was due to join me but he had not yet arrived. Sitting on a cold chair at the terminal, I double checked that my passport, tickets, and paraphernalia were with me. It had been a long time since I was this excited. I was about to go to where the Prophet Muhammad's [upon him be blessings and peace] story all began: Makkah.

The chaos of the terminal didn't bother me that day. My mind was on my destination and I was wondering what my emotions would be like when I first witnessed the ka'bah. This cuboid building in Makkah is shrouded in a black cloth and forms the heart of the city. The ka'bah marks the direction of prayer for Muslims the world over. It was the first mosque ever built—it was constructed by the Prophet Adam [upon him be peace]—and it existed long before the Prophet Muhammad [upon him be blessings and peace] was born.

God said, "Many a time We have seen you [Prophet] turn your face towards Heaven, so We are turning you towards a prayer direction that pleases you. Turn your face in the direction of the Sacred Mosque: wherever you [believers] may be, turn your faces to it. Those who were given the Scripture know with certainty that this is the Truth from their Lord: God is not unaware of what they do."[57]

How I longed to reach both Makkah and Madinah. The Prophet Muhammad's [upon him be blessings and peace] mosque and his grave were in Madinah. The word 'Madinah' means 'a city' in Arabic, and it is a shortened form of 'Madīnah al-Nabī', which meant 'The City of the Prophet'. His presence brings a sense of greatness to the city that no other city can rival. Madinah is the land of emigration, where the earliest Muslims went to after they were persecuted in their homeland of Makkah.

I wondered which city would appeal to me more. Almost everyone you speak to has their preference. Most likely Madinah, I thought, as nothing else of this world's pleasures could rival proximity to the Prophet Muhammad [upon him be blessings and peace] at his place of rest. Many of his family and companions [God be pleased with them] were also buried in Madinah. Moreover, Madinah was a place of refuge, a sanctuary for Muslims after they had endured torture and oppression. Madinah was a place of healing and growth.

My daydream was abruptly ended when I noticed my friend Awais walking towards me. Awais and I initially met through our mutual friend Subboor, who worked at iERA. Awais was a lawyer by profession but he had a strong love of da'wah and supported many projects. He was passionate about spreading the beautiful message of Islam to as many people as he could. Subboor, Awais, and I were good friends who often had dinner together to catch up with each other's lives and discuss both theology and worldly matters. Watching Subboor and Awais argue about whose city in Pakistan was better became a favourite pastime of mine.

Awais and I had a lot of catching up to do as we had not spoken to each other for a little while. We sat at a coffee shop and spoke over some bagels and coffee, keeping a close eye on the flight information board to see whether our gate number had shown up or not. I told Awais about all that had gone on in my life over the past months and how excited I was for this upcoming trip. We spoke about how much of a blessing it was and I mentioned how it wasn't something I planned long in advance but something that came up all of a sudden. The timing was perfect.

"Oh no!" interrupted Awais with a mortified expression as he stared at the information board. "What happened?" I replied. "The gate has closed." Our conversation had distracted us so much that Awais and I had forgotten to pay attention to the board. A spike of adrenaline rushed through us as we grabbed our bags and ran towards the gate. As I ran, I kept asking myself what would happen if I had ruined this opportune moment for myself.

We finally reached the gate, visibly anxious and out of breath, then we met the gate attendant, but he refused to let us on. "Sorry, guys. The gate is closed," said the attendant. We pleaded but the attendant said the plane was likely taxiing by now. Awais was already on the phone to the travel agent to check if another flight to Istanbul was available on the same day. His expression suggested the reply was in the negative. Our hotels had been booked and Awais had very limited time off from work in which he arranged this journey. The situation was dire.

I turned to God and prayed, "God, please make it happen." No sooner had I prayed than I noticed someone walking towards the gate attendants' desk and then having a conversation to him about us. After a few moments, the attendant approached us and said, "You guys are extremely lucky. You can go on."

For some reason I cannot now recall, the plane was delayed and needed to return to its gate. I vaguely remember the issue was to do with the baggage on the aircraft. This was the first miracle of the trip and it set the tone for the remainder of the journey. God was clearly watching over us.

Before long, we had arrived in Turkey and it was time to enter into a sacred state known as iḥrām. This is done by pilgrims wishing to visit Makkah and perform either a ḥajj [major pilgrimage] or ʿumrah [minor pilgrimage]. One is supposed to clean their body and wear two pieces of white cloth [women have different attire], one to cover the upper body and one to cover the lower body—a humble dress code.

I only had a short amount of time to get changed in a small cubicle we found at the Istanbul airport, but I remembered all the YouTube videos explaining the process. There are no buttons or zips on the pieces of white cloth and so one needs to fold them properly to keep them positioned well. It is strange to think that we wear normal clothes every day but never stop to be grateful for them. How useful are buttons, zips, stitches, and folds!

Entering the stage of iḥrām feels otherworldly. It feels as though you have left this lower world behind and reached a higher plane. All the male pilgrims were dressed in these white cloths and all around me was a sea of white. I could hear the talbiyyah being recited, "labbayk, Allahumma; labbayk. labbayka; lā sharīka laka labbayk. inna al-ḥamda wa niʿmata laka wa al-mulk. lā sharīka lak." ["At Your service, O Allah; at Your service. At Your service; You have no partner; at Your service. Truly all praise, favour, and sovereignty is Yours. You have no partner."].

We chanted this throughout the remainder of the flight and until we landed in Jeddah. Passing through security at Jeddah was a little difficult but we were soon through and sat inside a taxi on the way to our hotel. My knowledge of Arabic at the time was poor but thankfully Awais knew enough Arabic to help us get around.

We arrived in Makkah just before the dawn prayer. The darkness meant that I could not see much as I entered the city, other than scattered buildings and mountains surrounding the city's centre. As we approached the sacred mosque, a sense of peace began overwhelming my heart. We checked in at the hotel, which was within walking distance of the mosque, and then we headed straight to the mosque to catch the dawn prayer.

A lot of construction work was ongoing at the mosque and a temporary circular structure had been put in place to help enough people circumambulate the ka'bah whilst the construction work took place. Thousands of worshippers were in the mosque, all waiting for the call to stand up and pray. We found some space on the uppermost floor of the temporary structure surrounding ka'bah. I was eager to finally see the ka'bah with my own eyes for the first time. Rushing forward, I reached the front row. The ka'bah wasn't immediately visible as its roof was lower than where we were stood. I walked closer towards the ka'bah and then, suddenly, it came into view.

All I can remember of this moment was a huge sense of calm and serenity that overcame me when I saw the ka'bah. The din of thousands of worshippers around quietened in my mind and I felt as though I had reached the centre of the world, with the rest of the world wrapping around this point. Worshippers all around me were facing the centre, everyone looking at the ka'bah as if drawn to it by a powerful magnet at its core. My eyes did not move away from the ka'bah, and it was difficult to appreciate why this was the case when the structure was so simple. It was simple yet so mesmerising. It fel so serene and I didn't want to stop looking, but then the call for the morning prayer was announced and I needed to find a place to pray. This call to prayer assured me that I was truly there—this was not a dream.

The ka'bah is a wondrous place. It looked even more beautiful to me the following day under the light of the desert sun. It was a soul-rejuvenating sight and it almost felt as if I was learning to see all over again—but this time learning to see with something more than just my eyes. I began circumambulating around the ka'bah, something which every pilgrim does seven times, following the footsteps of the Prophet Abraham [upon him be peace]. Walking barefoot and a fair distance from the centre, this proved more difficult than I had anticipated. On around the third cycle, my feet began to blister, and by the sixth cycle, my feet felt as though they were on fire. I began to appreciate just how much of a blessing footwear is! That being said, it didn't bother me much at that moment, as my spiritual high proved a powerful anaesthetic. I was awestruck at how I was now walking in the same place the Prophet Muhammad [upon him be blessings and peace] had walked, performing the same ritual he had performed.

We then proceeded to the second stage of the 'umrah at the mountains of al-Ṣafā and al-Marwah. Pilgrims are tasked with walking between the two mountains seven times in emulation of the actions of Hagar [upon her be peace], the wife of the Prophet Abraham [upon him be peace]. She did so in search for aid as she was on the mountains in the desert heat with her thirst-stricken son Ishmael [upon him be peace]. Curiously, this practice of Muslims marks the only action of a major religious pilgrimage that is done in emulation of a woman and not a man. Hagar ran between the mountains and after her seventh journey, the Angel Gabriel [upon him be peace] struck the ground where Ishmael's foot hit it and water came gushing out.

So much water gushed out, in fact, that Hagar tried to stop it in fear that it would flood the region. She exclaimed, "Zam! Zam!" ["Gather! Gather!"], and so the well built there became known as the well of Zam Zam.

After completing the pilgrimage, men are tasked with shaving or cutting their hair—with shaving being preferable—and women are tasked with cutting their hair. I had never shaved my head before and was a little nervous over how I would look. Cutting is a possibility but considered less-than-ideal—I went all the way. Removing the hair, like all aspects of the pilgrimage, has a spiritual dimension. Shaving was a renewal and a sign that a pilgrim has completed the tasks assigned to him. I shaved my head and felt a powerful sense of relief wash through my body. The moment was overwhelming. Never before in my life had I felt those two contrasting emotions—feeling relieved and overwhelmed—at the same time so strongly.

This moment felt like a reset, a fresh start. With the shaving of my hair fell my ego, my arrogance, and my pride. I stood humbly before the Lord in two white cloths, physically exhausted but spiritually fresh. My identity and purpose were this—I was a worshipper. All the vain pursuits and public pretences I previously held on to were irrelevant. In chasing after things of no value, I had lost who I truly was. My true self was humble and my true purpose was noble. This revelation was incredibly freeing, and it brought along with it stillness, stability, and joy. God says, "And be not like those who forgot Allah, so He made them forget themselves. Those are the defiantly disobedient."[58]

Back at the hotel, I had a moment to myself to reflect on everything that had taken place thus far. The day had passed so quickly, it felt like a blur. Now, I had some time to rest and get a good night's sleep in the hotel, and that is exactly what I did.

When I woke up, we went to the breakfast buffet and had some surprisingly good food. It was especially enjoyable as we had a view that overlooked the surrounding mountains. These mountains had seen so much history unfold over the past millennia. "See those two mountains outside the window?" Awais asked. "Which ones?" I replied. Awais drew my attention to two mountains that were being levelled then said, "That's most likely where the Prophet [upon him be blessings and peace] once stood and addressed his people from. It's being cut through—probably to build new hotels."

Looking at the mountains, I couldn't help but thinking, this is exactly where the Prophet [upon him be blessings and peace] would have stood over 1,400 years ago. Looking around, I could see much more construction work taking place. We had a panorama view of our surroundings from the breakfast buffet, as there were glass windows all around. On the opposite side to the mountains, there were diggers and large drills, as well as cranes and trucks. To the left, a huge hole was being drilled through one of the mountains.

I asked Awais what was happening there and he replied that they were likely digging a tunnel for vehicles to pass through. These weren't the first tunnels being dug through the mountains of Makkah—that was, by now, a common occurrence. The words of ʿAbdullah ibn ʿAmr [God be pleased with him], a companion of the Prophet Muhammad [upon him be blessings and peace] came to mind. He said, "When you see tunnels/canals being dug in Makkah Mukarramah and the buildings higher than the mountain peaks, then know that Qiyāmah [The Day of Judgement] is near."[59]

The Prophet [upon him be blessings and peace] had told his Companions [God be pleased with them all] of many prophecies. Many have already come to pass and a few remain. Tall buildings were now common in Makkah and so were tunnels. I was sat in one of the tall buildings at the time. They were being built to accommodate the ever-increasing number of pilgrims that visited Makkah throughout the year.

After breakfast, we went to Jabal Nūr [The Mountain of Light], which was where the Prophet [upon him be blessings and peace] first received revelation from the Angel Gabriel [upon him be peace]. It was in a small cave at the top of this mountain—where the Prophet Muhammad [upon him be blessings and peace], in his younger years, would often sit, contemplate, and worship God—that it all began. Awais and I were eager to climb the mountain but my blistered feet from the day before were in no shape to do so.

We took a taxi to the base of the mountain and from there it was another 200 metres of steep incline walking before we would reach the cave. It felt much more difficult than it sounds, as the rough and jagged mountain terrain did not make for an easy ascent. The people descending seemed to be having an even harder time than those ascending. An old lady who had lost control of her descent came hurrying down the mountain. Her husband tried—but failed—to hold on to her. Thankfully, we were there to break her fall and prevent her injuring herself. The couple was very grateful.

I asked Awais how these elderly people were reaching the cave given their frailty and he replied saying that they would not reach the cave but would just go as far as they could and then return—people did what they could. Reaching the cave is not a mandatory part of any pilgrimage, but for some people it is an expression of love and reverence. Even at the foot of the mountain I felt breathless and unfit, but I was determined that I would not let sore feet or an under-serviced cardiovascular system stop me from reaching the cave.

Steps had been carved into the mountain to make it easier for people wanting to climb. Along the way up, there were rest areas. Some people would rest and continue ascending, whilst others would ascend and then return down the mountain. Lots of monkeys inhabited the mountains and I was warned not to go near them as they may attack. It was a good thing I was told this as I was about to approach a trio of adorable-looking monkeys to interact with them. Mind you, they only looked adorable until one of them 'smiled' at me, bearing his sharp teeth.

It was soon going to be sunset and we needed to hurry up. We were about halfway up when I got so tired that I needed a break. Awais is a little older than me but he was managing without much difficulty. As we rested, we noticed a man dressed in white shalwar kameez—the national dress of Pakistan—and smiling. He was carrying two large bags and showed no signs of tiredness. "He's from Murree," said Awais, referring to a mountainous region of Pakistan that our friend Subboor was also from. Awais was sure of it due to how easy the man was finding the climb. Within moments, the man had ascended to reach where we were sat and so Awais asked him where he was from. To Awais' delight, it turned out the man was from Murree! After a brief conversation, the man continued his ascend and we followed just behind him.

We reached the summit of the mountain just as the sun had begun to set andt he area was flooded with people trying to enter the small cave. We stood back for a moment, just trying to take in both our surroundings and the majesty of the location, noticing that the cave itself was tiny, with just enough space for one person to sit in. Prior to this, I had always imagined that it would be a large cave with lots of room. We sat outside the cave—the cave in which the Prophet Muhammad [upon him be blessings and peace] would sit in seclusion from the world and meditate. This cave was where he was when the first revelation came down.

It had been a long time since I had thought about or read about the Prophet Muhammad [upon him be blessings and peace]. This upset me a great deal. This man was the one to whom revelation descended, and he gave up a comfortable life to spread the word of God. He was attacked both physically and verbally, but that did not stop him fighting tirelessly and allowing people like myself to receive the message so many years later. The Prophet's [upon him be blessings and peace] character was one of the things that had convinced me of Islam those many years ago. God said to the Prophet [upon him be blessings and peace], "And indeed, you are of a great moral character."[60]

This spectacular moment atop the Mountain of Light was much needed, as after such a long time, I was again struck by the greatness of the Prophet Muhammad [upon him be blessings and peace], the most beautiful man to have ever lived and the most beloved of God. Prior to revelation, his people loved him greatly and referred to him as al-Ṣādiq al-Amīn [The Truthful One, The Trustworthy One], then when revelation descended and he advised his people to fear God worshipping only Him, and abandoning all vices—such as female infanticide, cheating in business, and appropriating the wealth of orphans—that would bring about His displeasure, most of the people turned against him. It was through love, empathy, preaching, and the miracle of prophethood that he convinced so many people, but change takes time and he suffered a great deal throughout his mission.

His love was generous and reached people, animals, plants, and even the inanimate world. He did not deny those who asked for his help. He did not waver in his mission ever. Words struggle to do him justice, but I do love the following poem written by the iERA team:

A man who taught mercy,

Kindness and duty;

A man who repelled evil with

Virtue and beauty.

A man who brought forgiveness

And inspired the truth;

A man who dispelled racism

And was never aloof.

A man who sought justice

And the end of oppression;

A man who was forbearing

Through trial and repression.

A man who loved orphans

And supported the weak;

A man who gave life to the

Rights that we seek.

A man with compassion

And loving grace;

A man who smiled

At every face.

A man who affirmed and

Taught God's Divinity;

A man who inspired hope

And endless serenity.

A man who was upright,

Honest and kind;

He was the prophet Muhammad,

A mercy to mankind.[61]

That evening on the mountain was another landmark moment in my life. Reconnecting with the Prophet Muhammad [upon him be blessings and peace] was something I needed to do and having the opportunity to do so upon the Mountain of Light was an incredible blessing. God says, "And We have not sent you, [O Muhammad], except as a mercy to the worlds."[62]

During the next couple of days in Makkah, I spent a lot of time at the mosque resting on the cool marble flooring, contemplating my life and soul searching whilst admiring the ka'bah—a building I could not stop staring at. I asked God to heal me. However, I did not ask for an immediate solution, as I had, by now, learned just how beneficial the moments of suffering proved for my development, and I was confident that I would heal in time and that whatever remnants of distress I was feeling would leave me when they had served their purpose. I implored God to give me patience. The environment around me had changed the way I saw the world—I was much more optimistic around the ka'bah than I was elsewhere.

Two important factors had led to this change in me. First, I realised just how un-special I was. Around me were thousands of slaves of God who were just as valuable as me and who were doing exactly what I was doing, meaning that life could not possibly revolve around me, my wishes, and my problems. Second, I felt incredibly blessed that I was in a position professionally through which I could share the message of Islam with the world. This opportunity was not given to many and it was something I needed to be grateful for. Reflecting on these two points shifted my thoughts to far more optimistic ones.

Never before in my life had I really appreciated the value of optimism. During my second crisis, I would be optimistic on occasion, but would be in despair most of the time. Optimism opens the doors of mercy and brings about the love of God; pessimism leads to ingratitude and a downward spiral of emotions. In the first instance, every Muslim should think well of God. The Prophet Muhammad [upon him be blessings and peace] once said, "Indeed Allah, the Most High, says, 'I am as My slave thinks of Me, and I am with him when He calls upon Me.'"[63]

Often during moments of tragedy, our 'Problem of Evil' thoughts are, in fact, problems with our opinions of God. We take the harshness and difficulty of a moment and use that to try and tear down what was otherwise so logically clear and spiritually evident to us. Without accepting our inability to comprehend God's wisdom, and without being patient for God's justice in the world to come, and without accepting that we only know what we know through God's permission, we begin to accuse God of being unjust—may God protect us from doing so ever again.

We must be vigilant over our hearts and protect them from the clouds of pessimism and ingratitude, as if we do not, we risk deluding ourselves into thinking that our emotional and moral judgements are logical ones and not just our struggling to cope with difficult situations. We lose sight of the blessings that we have—our ability to reason, for one!—and a veil begins to cover our eyes. This veil stops us seeing the love of God and his generosity. It stops us realising that every trial is just that and that our Lord wants us to constantly improve.

How we view the world is up to us. Our opinions are subjective and are influenced by what surrounds us, what has occurred, and what space we allow our minds to inhabit. Things happen in our lives and we have a choice in how we frame these things and how we respond to them. We can see the truth of things as they are or we can choose to hate and complain. Looking back, my second crisis was full of moments in which I thought that God was punishing me—in those moments I felt the lowest. At those low points, instead of seeing the opportunity in the hardship, I began pitying myself and was unwilling to take the necessary actions to fix my internal issues.

I realised that when my thoughts were positive, I was at my most productive and my recovery sped up; I entered an upwards spiral. Even though it took me a while to learn this, I am glad I did, and ever since I have held a more positive understanding of God and His mercy, my life has been so much happier.

Our trip to Makkah was coming to a close and I made my last visit to the mosque just before we left for Madinah. I was leaving one sanctuary to visit another. The drive in the taxi to Madinah was around four-and-a-half hours long through a beautiful desert and there was nothing but the desert and mountains all around—it was unadultered, beautiful nature that surrounded us. The taxi driver and Awais began speaking. It turned out that the taxi driver had worked for the Saudi royal family at one point in his life. He began mentioning the prophecies of the Prophet Muhammad [upon him be blessings and peace], one of which was his saying, "The Hour will not come… till the land of Arabia reverts to meadows and rivers."[64]

This prophecy was beginning to come to pass back then, and nowadays the case is even more so, with actual meadows in parts of Arabia. Recent research has shown that Arabia once had lush and fertile plains, including a 2014 article published by the BBC which described a team of agroecologists from Oxford who uncovered tusks belonging to an elephant that had lived 325,000 years ago in the Saudi desert.[65] The experts averred that this was solid proof that the desert of Arabia was once a land of fertile grounds upon which many animals roamed.

As the driver and Awais continued to speak, I remembered a dream I had about a year earlier in which the ka'bah was surrounded by greenery, as if it were sat in a field on a warm summer day. Crystal clear water was flowing under the ka'bah, which was propped up on four pillars. This dream was incredibly vivid and I have never forgotten it. What struck me about the dream was that I had it before I had ever known about this narration and before I had made any plans to visit Makkah. Perhaps in this dream were good tidings from God of my eventual visit to Makkah.

Whatever the case, both the dream and the conversation between Awais and the taxi driver made me reflect over the truthful nature of the Prophet [upon him be blessings and peace]. Now, I was on my way to visit the Prophet Muhammad's [upon him be blessings and peace] mosque and his grave—the greatest man who ever lived.

CHAPTER 11

MADINAH

By the time we reached Madinah, the sun had set. Madinah had a palpably different atmosphere to Makkah. Makkah was busy and majestic; Madinah was beautiful and peaceful. Madinah was also far more developed as a city. We checked into our hotel, quickly freshened up, then went straight to the al-Masjid al-Nabawī [The Prophet's Mosque]. When it was first built, the mosque was a very simple structure that was linked to the Prophet's [upon him be blessings and peace] modest house. 1,400 years later, the mosque had become a huge and grand mosque. In fact, the new mosque is bigger than the whole main city of Madinah used to be.

As we walked towards the mosque, a huge sense of peace overcame me, just as it had done in Makkah. The Prophet Muhammad [upon him be blessings and peace] migrated to Madinah after 13 very difficult years of delivering the message of Islam to the people of Makkah. God inspired him to leave and his journey was a thing of wonder, combining the precariousness of human nature with the awesomeness of divine protection. Some of the Makkans had tried to kill him before he left for Madinah. When they failed, they tried to kill him during his journey.

Our journey to Madinah was a lot easier! We walked into the mosque from the entrance furthest from the Prophet's [upon him be blessings and peace] grave. The mosque was so beautiful—I had never seen anything quite like it before, with its beautiful arches, the marble pillars, the symmetry, and the subtle design elements that all appeared so mesmerising. Standing under an arch, one could see hundreds of other, similar arches, as if one was looking into an infinity mirror. Intricately embroidered red carpets furnished the marble floors. Some worshippers were sat reclined against the pillars, some were sat on the carpets, and some were asleep on the floors. Some people were reciting the Qur'ān out loud, some were reciting quietly, and some were focusing on other things.

People who could not afford to stay in hotels close to the mosque often spent the whole day inside the mosque, even taking naps there. Elderly people, especially, would rest in the mosque to regain energy. Many people save money for decades to afford the journey to Makkah and Madinah; their hearts overflow with love from the moment they begin their journey to the moment they leave the holy sites. It really put into perspective how silly many of my own complaints and niggles were. I was staying in a 4/5-starred hotel very close to the mosque and still managed to complain about how tired I felt.

As we walked through the mosque, we could hear the Qur'ān being recited around us. We were walking towards the Prophet's [upon him be blessings and peace] grave. It had been more than 1,400 years since he left the world, but the result of his call to God was still being felt the world over. Every year, more and more people were embracing Islam and studying his life and message. The mere fact that his religion was still growing despite him having lived in such a different time, and that it had never stopped growing, was a miracle in itself. God says, "[Prophet], do you not see how God makes comparisons? A good word is like a good tree whose root is firm and whose branches are high in the sky, yielding constant fruit by its Lord's leave—God makes such comparisons for people so that they may reflect—but an evil word is like a rotten tree, uprooted from the surface of the earth, with no power to endure."[66]

The Prophet Muhammad [upon him be blessings and peace] claimed that he was a prophet of God. Immediately, he was believed by his wife Khadījah [God be pleased with her] and best friend, Abū Bakr [God be pleased with him]. Others took longer to accept the message, initially rejecting it and then being compelled through their intellects and hearts to accept it. All of us have to make the same decision: to believe or reject the message. The Prophet [upon him be blessings and peace] had nothing in sight to gain materially from spreading his message. He and his followers suffered from intense physical and emotional punishment due to their beliefs and He was exiled from his homeland. At one point, he was effectively offered the world—women, wealth, and power—if he stopped preaching, yet he continued to preach. He worshipped fervently, with the night prayer made obligatory upon him. He gave to charity and lived an incredibly difficult life. He chose poverty even when wealth began flooding into the hands of the Muslims, and no two consecutive nights passed in Madinah in which hot food was made in his house. He was known as the 'The Truthful One, The Trustworthy One'. Why would he lie?

I've never met anybody who would wake up one day and just start speaking complete lies after having spent 40 years of their lives building a reputation among their community for their honesty and trustworthiness. Even more bizarre would be for one who lived a life of relative ease to make up these lies and continue to hold on to them, even if they brought repeated harm to them, and even if this person was offered multiple opportunities to get out of harm's way.

He was obviously not a liar. Was he, then, deluded? A deluded person, definitionally, has lost touch with reality. It is an indication of madness and insanity. But the Prophet Muhammad [upon him be blessings and peace] was extremely coherent, very rational in his approach, and very much in touch with reality. His understanding of people and spirituality was clear. He was an excellent politician and unparalleled public speaker. He never spoke in a delusional manner. His words were well thought out and deeply meaningful. His speeches were full of wisdom and empathy.

Deluded people jump on any occurrence which may support their position. The Prophet Muhammad [upon him be blessings and peace] was not like this either. On the same day his son Abraham [God be pleased with him] passed away, there was an eclipse in Arabia. People began speaking and saying it was due to the death of the Prophet's [upon him be blessings and peace] son. A deluded man would have jumped on this opportunity, at least in his own mind. The Prophet Muhammad [upon him be blessings and peace], however, responded by saying, "The sun and the moon do not eclipse because of the death or life [i.e. birth] of someone. When you see the eclipse pray and invoke Allah."[67]

He was obviously not deluded. Even those who knew him but rejected his messaged conceded that he was not a liar nor was he deluded. Many accused him of being a magician, but even those accusations fell flat. Eventually, Arabia became completely Muslim—everyone around believing in his message almost without exception. Now, Islam has spread to 1,800,000,000 people worldwide—that many Muslims around the globe all believing in what he brought. Many of these Muslims believe in Islam simply through the character and story of the Prophet Muhammad [upon him be blessings and peace].

Eventually, we made it to the grave of the Prophet Muhammad [upon him be blessings and peace]. We slowly walked forwards among a crowd of people until we walked past the rawḍah [garden]—which was a green-carpeted area of the mosque that the Prophet Muhammad [upon him be blessings and peace] referred to as being one of the gardens of Paradise. People queue for a long time just to get an opportunity to pray there.

As I approached the grave of the Prophet Muhammad [upon him be blessings and peace], I could see it was surrounded by black and gold gates which, themselves, surrounded an internal brick structure. The grave was behind there, hidden from our view. Musk and rose scent filled the air and there was a sense of love and reverence around the grave. It was difficult to believe just how close I was standing to the Prophet Muhammad [upon him be blessings and peace]. My emotions at that place are beyond words. This was physically the closest I would be to him in my life. I cannot imagine how his companions [God be pleased with them all] must have felt being so close to him.

A man who was opposed to the Prophet Muhammad [upon him be blessings and peace] once observed him with his companions and then returned to his own people, saying, "O people! By Allah, I have been to the kings and to Caesar, Khosrau, and the Negus, yet I have never seen any of them respected by their courtiers as much as Muhammad is respected by his companions. By Allah, if he spat, the spittle would fall in the hand of one of them [i.e. the Prophet's companions] who would rub it on his face and skin; if he ordered them, they would carry out his order immediately; if he performed ablution, they would struggle to take the remaining water; and when they spoke, they would lower their voices and would not look at his face constantly out of respect."[68]

Yet he was humble and shy. He avoided pageantry and pomp. He lived modestly and would sit among the people. He loved the poor and hated ostentation. He wore simple clothes and ate simple food. He was like this throughout his life.

As I thought about the Prophet Muhammad [upon him be blessings and peace], a thread of sadness and longing entered my mind, as I wished that he was here with us, guiding us in these troubled times. I lamented over how we did not have his companionship and how distant we were in time, but as I was thinking this, the sound of the Qurʾān being recited entered my ears and I realised we were not left without a guide. We have the Qurʾān—a guide for all times. In fact, the Prophet Muhammad's [upon him be blessings and peace] character was based on the Qurʾān. Someone once asked his wife ʿĀʾishah [God be pleased with her] about his character and she replied, "Have you not read the Qurʾān?" They responded, "Of course," to which ʿĀʾishah remarked, "Truly, the character of the Prophet of Allah [upon him be blessings and peace] was the Qurʾān."[69] At this realisation, my desire to learn Arabic and truly engage with the Qurʾān heightened.

I managed to get a few opportunities to pray in the rawḍah, another unforgettable experience. Prostrating on the same ground that the Prophet Muhammad [upon him be blessings and peace] prostrated on was an other-worldly moment. During the trip, these spiritually intense moments were relatively commonplace. They brought a certain conviction of faith to my heart that penetrated deeper than any rational proof ever could, and they really helped me understand that belief is not purely an intellectual phenomenon. We are tasked with using our intellects to reason and believe, but our intellects are not the only reason—nor even the primary reason—we believe. Belief is a gift from God given to those who open their hearts to him, those he favours.

This trip had come at the perfect time for me. I was able to reconcile a lot that had taken place in my life and put everything into perspective. Back in London, I reflected and wrote down some of the key lessons I learned, which made it very clear to me that us humans are prone to becoming deluded and lost in self-amazement if we are not careful. This can lead to one worshipping one's own self. Further, this reflection meant that I had developed an appreciation for the many different dimensions to Islam. Prior to this experience, faith in my mind was all about rational discussions and intellectual debates. It was now clear to me that there is a time for rational discussions but that faith is something experienced—it is something that one tastes the sweetness of. Practising Islam as it should be practiced brings with it this sweetness and certainty.

CHAPTER 12

THE LANGUAGE OF THE QUR'ĀN

Perhaps the most visible change in my behaviour following my trip to the two holy mosques was in how I engaged with the Qur'ān. My epiphany at the Prophet Muhammad's [upon him be blessings and peace] mosque had left a deep impression upon me and I now wanted to learn Arabic and understand the Qur'ān directly, not through the attempted translation of another man. I wanted to experience, first-hand, the miracle experienced by the Arabs around the Prophet Muhammad [upon him be blessings and peace]. It was a miracle that left them speechless and stunned, even the sternest of his opponents felt it. Those who rallied against him during the day would leave their beds and go in secret to hear him recite the Qur'ān during the night.

There are many miracles in the Qur'ān. Many of them I had already studied and was convinced of. It was the simple truths that really affected me, truths about the preservation of the Qur'ān and the conservation of its message. How could a book so old be preserved so perfectly? I couldn't think of any other example of this happening in the world. And this phenomenon was not due to chance. God said, "We have sent down the Quran Ourself, and We Ourself will guard it."[70]

Another miracle of the Qur'ān is found in the timelessness of its message. Even through a translation, it speaks directly to so many people and it changes people's lives across the world and across time, responding to the problems of man and giving every one of us direction. The Qur'ān never disappoints, and how could it, when it is the word of God?

I looked into different Arabic courses and realised that there were a number of different types of Arabic dialects that one could learn. These differed depending on one's aims in learning the language. There was Modern Standard Arabic, Formal Arabic, and Classical Arabic, as well as regional dialects. The choice made me reflect on why I wanted to learn Arabic in the first place. It was to understand the Qur'ān, and with this in mind, I chose Classical Arabic and knew I would need to focus on studying Arabic grammar. My dyslexia did not make it easy, but I was persistent. I bought books on Arabic grammar and studied these whilst searching for courses to take up.

The first few weeks of my Arabic journey were difficult. I had struggled with English grammar and spelling all my life and now I needed to learn these things in another language, but as I persisted, things began to fall into place. Arabic seemed to have a deeply mathematical structure as an agglutinative language, making its rules easier to remember. Eventually, I found an evening Arabic course at the University of London, SOAS. Without hesitation, I joined the year-long course, which was excellent, and through persistent attendance, the rules of grammar were becoming increasingly clear to me.

Grammar without vocabulary does not a language make. I appreciated I was making progress, but I was extremely keen to improve my vocabulary and be able to comprehend the Qur'ān directly. Learning vocabulary was going to take longer than learning grammar did and vocabulary-only courses don't seem to exist.

After deliberating, I decided to first learn the words of the Qur'ān. I downloaded some mobile apps and found a couple of lexicons then made a start, before realising something amazing. The Qur'ān has approximately 78,000 words within it and they all stem from approximately 1,700 root words. This made familiarising oneself with the Book much easier, making me optimistic; but then I hit another wall. My brain was not wired for the rote memorisation of lists of words. No matter how hard I tried, I seemed to keep on forgetting the words I had previously learned.

Usefully, I came across an Urdu commentary on the Qur'ān by a scholar named Farhat Hashmi which was unique as her focus was specifically on the vocabulary of the Qur'ān. I listened to her commentary and held a copy of the Qur'ān as I did so, reading along as the commentary moved on. Returning to my studies the next day, I decided to read through the verses I had covered with the Hashmi commentary and, to my surprise, I had remembered the meanings of the words! I was reading the Arabic without a translation and it was making sense to me. I repeated this process later that day and the same result repeated itself the next day—I was able to comprehend the Arabic.

I realised that learning the meanings and contexts of words was incredibly important in aiding memorisation, and this amazing breakthrough allowed me to memorise vocabulary, practice using my grammar rules, and learn more about the meanings of the Qur'ān.

The more I learned, the more I realised there was to learn, and the more I appreciated that I was a beginner on a long road of pious and humble study. Over the next couple of years, my Arabic skills improved greatly and I had reached the point where I could open any page of the Qur'ān and comprehend 70-80% of what was being said. This was a huge achievement for me and my appreciation for the depth of the Qur'ān grew immensely as a result. I began to realise just how much was lost in translation and how many of the subtleties I had missed before.

The progression from my reliance upon translations to my ability to directly read and understand the Qur'ān evoked within me a desire to share the miracle of the Qur'ān's language with the world. I wondered how I could get those who did not speak Arabic to appreciate this miracle. Hamza Tzortzis worked on this problem and came up with an argument he referred to as "God's testimony." He refined this argument to the point where everyone, Arabic-speaker and non-Arabic speaker, could appreciate the miracle of the Qur'ān.

In his book The Divine Reality, after a short discussion on the philosophy of testimony and inference to the best explanation, he outlined his argument as follows [before delving into a more detailed discussion]:

P1: The Qur'ān presents a literary and linguistic challenge to humanity [God asks humanity to reproduce even a single chapter like one of its chapters if they believe it is from other than God].

P2: The 7th century Arabs—who were masters of the language—were best placed to challenge the Qur'ān.

P3: The 7th century Arabs failed to do so.

P4: Scholars of the Arabic language have testified to the Qur'ān's inimitability.

P5: Counter-scholarly testimonies are implausible, as they need to reject the established background information.

C1: Therefore, the Qur'ān is inimitable.

P6: The possible explanations for the Qur'ān's inimitability are: authorship by an Arab, authorship by a non-Arab, or authorship by God.

P7: It could not have been produced by an Arab or a non-Arab.

C2: Therefore, the best explanation is that the Qur'ān is from God.[71]

Following this, Hamza elaborated on each of these points and explains how they are not reasonably contestable. The Arabs at the time of revelation had the most beautiful Arabic of all people, being famed for their linguistic prowess and indulging in poetry as a communal pastime. These Arabs were in the best position to refute the Qur'ān's challenge, had it been possible to do so. God said, "Say, 'Even if all mankind and jinn came together to produce something like this Quran, they could not produce anything like it, however much they helped each other.'"[72] God also said, "If they say, 'He has invented it himself,' say, 'Then produce ten invented sūrahs like it, and call in whoever you can beside God, if you are truthful.'"[73] God also said, "If you have doubts about the revelation We have sent down to Our servant, then produce a single sūrah like it—enlist whatever supporters you have other than God—if you are truthful."[74] God also said, "Or do they say, 'He has devised it'? Say, 'Then produce a sūrah like it, and call on anyone you can beside God if you are telling the truth.'"[75]

This challenge was not hidden, and it was put forward to the best Arab linguists of all time. Even if one was to entertain the idea that the Prophet Muhammad [upon him be blessings and peace] forged the Qur'ān, why would he risk being exposed by offering so brazen a challenge to a community of Arabs who were expert linguists? The smallest sūrah of the Qur'ān is 10 words long. Why make the challenge so 'easy' if this were a forgery?

There is an unwavering confidence in the language of the Qur'ān, a godly confidence. Many people tried to imitate the Qur'ān and they all failed. The best of the poets in Arabia were asked by their people to take up the challenge. Among them was al-Walīd ibn al-Mughīrah. Ibn ʿAbbās narrated that, "al-Walīd ibn al-Mughīrah [a polytheist] came to the Messenger of Allah [upon him be blessings and peace]. The Messenger of Allah [upon him be blessings and peace] recited the Qur'ān to him, and al-Walīd seemed to become affected and softened by it. Abū Jahl came to know of this, so he came to al-Walīd and said, 'Don't you see that your people are collecting charity for you?' He said, 'And why is that?' Abū Jahl replied, 'So that they can give it to you, as they see that you went to Muhammad to get some of his food.' al-Walīd said, 'Quraysh knows that I am of the wealthiest of its sons.' Abū Jahl said, 'So, say to Muhammad something that would convince your people that you oppose him.' al-Walīd replied, 'And what can I possibly say? There is not a single man who is more knowledgeable of poetry or prose than I, even the poetry of the jinn, and by Allah, what he says bears no resemblance to these things. By Allah, what he says has a sweetness to it and a charm upon it; the highest part of it is fruitful and the lowest part of it is gushing forth with bounty; it dominates and cannot be dominated, and it crushes all that is under it.'"[76]

Since then, many have tried to meet this challenge and all have failed embarrassingly. The Arabs at the time of revelation who were opposed to the message gave up trying to challenge the Qur'ān linguistically. Instead, they tried to kill the Messenger [upon him be blessings and peace] with their swords. This much is testified to by many scholars and experts, both Muslims and non-Muslims, from the past to the present. Edward Palmer, for example, wrote, "that the best of Arab writers has never succeeded in producing anything equal in merit to the Qur'an itself is not surprising."[77]

CHAPTER 13

GRATITUDE

A few years ago, whilst on holiday in Pakistan, I fed a starving and injured dog. I gave him whatever bits of food I could find and he devoured it all within moments. Afterwards, he followed me around and would not leave me alone. Eventually, he came towards my feet, rolled over onto his back, and began wagging his tail. Till this day, I cannot forget the love I saw in his eyes when he stared at me, as it had caught me off-guard and left me speechless. It was his way of showing gratitude and it was a connection that I relish even now.

Gratitude is an intrinsic characteristic of humanity. We cannot help but to give thanks when someone is good to us. Gratitude is so central to our wellbeing that psychotherapists now utilise exercises in gratitude to help overcome depression and other ailments.

Gratitude is necessary. We thank each other but always remember that praise ultimately belongs to God. The Prophet Muhammad [upon him be peace] once said, "He who does not thank people does not thank God."[78] I am thankful to all those who helped me along my journey and all those who are yet to help me. I remain a work in progress and hope that I become a better person each day. There was a time in my life in which I felt like I was God's gift to the world. Now, I feel more like I an explorer searching through God's gift of the world.

There is so much beauty around us and all of it is teleological. As I grow in life and raise my children, I hope that they are able to appreciate these things, understanding that this life is a test and that tests aren't always easy, but that we have a merciful and untiring Lord who helps us along the way. We just need to humble ourselves, submit ourselves to Him, and persevere along the path He set for us. God has no need of us; we have complete need of Him.

As we bring this book to a close, it is important that we remember why it was written in the first place. I wished to tell my story, pour my heart out, invite to God's way, and give thanks to my merciful Lord who has saved me from the depths of despair. It feels appropriate to relate the translation of the opening chapter of the Qur'ān at this point. God says,

"In the name of Allah, the Merciful, the Mercifier.

Praise belongs to Allah, Lord of the Worlds, the Merciful, the Mercifier, Master of the Day of Judgement. It is You we worship; it is You we ask for help. Guide us to the straight path: the path of those upon whom You have bestowed favour, not of those who have earned [Your] anger or of those who are astray."[79]

EPILOGUE

This book was written for those who have become aware that there is more to life than meets the eye, for those who have begun to ponder over life's deeper question, and for those who have fallen into internal crises from which they are struggling to escape. Sharing my journey, laying out my flaws and insecurities, was not an easy task. However, writing everything out made me realise just how much I have grown through the trauma I endured. Had it not been for the hardships I faced, I would not be the person I am now and this book would not have existed. Indeed, my trials were a gift whose blessings continue to manifest till this day.

I am aware that there are many people across the world that are going through the difficulties that I went through, and that they have endured similar experiences to those I have shared. Some may even be suffering more than I did. If you are one of those people, then know that you are not alone. The deep questions you are mulling over are questions that have occurred to a great multitude of people before you. Even those you wouldn't suspect—all the normal people you see everyday as you live your life—would have thought about these questions at some point in their lives. Some people are more easily distracted by the world and try to forget these questions or pretend they aren't real questions in the first place. If you are not one of these people, then consider yourself to be among the fortunate. God is giving you a chance to approach Him.

If you have reached this point of enquiry, then it is time to open your mind and listen to your heart. Remove the veil imposed by the world and its distractions and allow your paradigm to shift. Doggedly trying to find an intellectual solution for your conundrum whilst remaining within an atheistic and naturalistic paradigm will not work, as those necessarily preclude and obfuscate any notion of the Divine. You may already be aware of this—aware of the fact that something doesn't quite make sense. Were you to allow yourself to believe that, perhaps, God does exist, then the world would make complete sense. Until you accept this, your choices will be only to remain in suffering or to veil the suffering and leap into the world and its material distractions.

Despite whatever you have done in the past, whatever hardships you have faced, and whatever you have thought about God and religion, the door to God's mercy remains open. We must not allow our suffering to make us irrationally angry with God. Nor must we allow this anger to obscure our reasoning. Humans do not like pain and suffering. Our brains think in very short terms and we have great difficulty in understanding infinite. God is greater. He has made the world in such a way that difficulty, suffering, and hardship are allowed to be a part of it. He has promised us ultimate justice in the Hereafter and has tasked us with spreading as much goodness—as well as warding off as much harm—as we can in this world. If you appreciate the honour you have been granted through this mission, love will overcome you.

Islam is a religion that defines its followers as those who submit wholeheartedly to God. In this submission does one find freedom, peace, and stability. My own story shows how I found these things through my acceptance of the faith. I became a better, more productive person and every existential question I had was answered for me. It wasn't an easy journey to get to that point, and the hardest part of the journey was to lower my guard, humble myself, and rid myself of all arrogance. God loves the humble-hearted and the humble-hearted love God.

I bear witness that there is no God but Allah, and I bear witness that Muhammad [upon him be blessings and peace] is the Messenger of Allah.

Endnotes

1   Harris S. Waking Up. Simon and Schuster; 2014.

2   Hamza Andreas Tzortzis. The Divine Reality: God, Islam & the Mirage of Atheism. Hong Kong: Lion Rock Publishing; 2019.

3   Marino GD. Basic Writings of Existentialism. New York: Modern Library; 2004.

4   In the chapter "Existential Angst," Albert Camus is referred to but no reference is given.

5   Camus A. The Myth of Sisyphus. London: Penguin, Cop; 2005.

6   al-Qurʾān 13:28.

7   Kasser T. The High Price of Materialism. Cambridge, Mass.: MIT Press; 2002.

8   al-Qurʾān 112:1-4.

9   al-Qurʾān 51:56.

10   al-Qurʾān 95:4.

11   al-Qurʾān 17:70.

12   al-Qurʾān 67:1-2.

13   al-Qurʾān 3:12.

14   al-Qurʾān 31:8.

15   al-Qurʾān 25:43.

16   al-Qurʾān 20:124.

17   al-Qurʾān 7:146.

18   al-Qurʾān 7:146.

19   al-Qurʾān 113:1.

20   Ali A. English Tafseer Chapter 113 Surah Al-Falaq. Available from: www.quran.live

21   al-Qurʾān 2:74.

22   al-Qurʾān 40:60.

23   The Bible, Matthew 26:39.

24 al-Qurʾān 48:4.

25 al-Qurʾān 112:1-4.

26 Pickthall M. The Meaning of the Glorious Koran. 1930.

27 al-Qurʾān 36:82.

28 Hume D. Dialogues Concerning Natural Religion. S.L.: Bibliotech Press; 2019.

29 Rizvi AA. The Atheist Muslim. St. Martin's Press; 2016.

30 al-Qurʾān 67:2.

31 Dostoevsky F. The Brothers Karamazov. Penguin Classics. 2024.

32 al-Qurʾān 21:23.

33 Sunan Ibn Mājah 4013.

34 Ṣaḥīḥ Muslim 2999.

35 al-Qurʾān 18:66.

36 al-Qurʾān 18:67-68.

37 al-Qurʾān 18:70.

38 al-Qurʾān 18:69-82.

39 al-Qurʾān 52:35-36.

40 al-Qurʾān 2:186.

41 Reichenbach B. Cosmological Argument (Stanford Encyclopedia of Philosophy) [Internet]. Stanford.edu. 2017. Available from: https://plato.stanford.edu/entries/cosmological-argument/

42 al-Qurʾān 22:46.

43 al-Qurʾān 39:53.

44 University O. Humans "predisposed" to believe in gods and the afterlife [Internet]. phys.org. 2011. Available from: https://phys.org/news/2011-05-humans-predisposed-gods-afterlife.html

45 Raatikainen P. Gödel's Incompleteness Theorems (Stanford Encyclopedia of Philosophy) [Internet]. Stanford.edu. 2013. Available from: https://plato.stanford.edu/entries/goedel-incompleteness/

46 Raatikainen P. Gödel's Incompleteness Theorems (Stanford Encyclopedia of Phi-

losophy) [Internet]. Stanford.edu. 2013. Available from: https://plato.stanford.edu/entries/goedel-incompleteness/

47 Craver C, Tabery J. Mechanisms in Science [Internet]. Summer 2019. Zalta EN, editor. Stanford Encyclopedia of Philosophy. Metaphysics Research Lab, Stanford University; 2019. Available from: https://plato.stanford.edu/entries/science-mechanisms/

48 Chapman A. Isaac Newton Philosophiae naturalis principia mathematica Authorised by the Royal Society, 5th July 1686; published, London, 1687. [Internet]. Ox.ac.uk. 2024 [cited 2024 Jul 26]. Available from: https://library.wadham.ox.ac.uk/exhibition/newton.html

49 Chomsky's Philosophy. Noam Chomsky on René Descartes [Internet]. YouTube. 2017 [cited 2024 Jul 26]. Available from: https://www.youtube.com/watch?v=EVFBABFdLXE&t=12s&ab_channel=Chomsky%27sPhilosophy

50 al-Qur'ān 30:54.

51 Harrell E. Out of the Depths: An Unforgettable WWII Story of Survival, Courage, and the Sinking of the USS Indianapolis. Bethany House Publishers; 2016.

52 Hamilton D. Preparing for Shipwreck. Camp Hill Church of Christ. Year unknown [cited 2024 Jul 26].

53 "God himself could not sink this ship." The Titanic, Bruce Ismay and Trump [Internet]. The Inglorius Padre Steve's World. 2020. Available from: https://padresteve.com/2020/04/15/god-himself-could-not-sink-this-ship-the-titanic-bruce-ismay-and-trump/

54 Turner S. The band that played on : the extraordinary story of the 8 musicians who went down with the Titanic. Nashville, Tenn.: Thomas Nelson; 2011.

55 al-Qur'ān 31:31-32.

56 al-Qur'ān 19:22-26.

57 al-Qur'ān 2:144.

58 al-Qur'ān 59:19.

59 Muṣannaf ibn Abī Shaybah 14306.

60 al-Qur'ān 68:4.

61 Muhammad: Mercy To Mankind Campaign [Internet]. iera.ca. [cited 2024 Jul 27]. Available from: https://iera.ca/our-work/campaigns/mercy-campaign/

62 al-Qur'ān 21:107.

63   Jāmiʿ al-Tirmidhī 2388.

64   Ṣaḥīḥ Muslim 157c.

65   Gardner F. Tusk clue to Saudi desert's green past. BBC News [Internet]. 2014 Apr 2 [cited 2024 Jul 27]; Available from: https://www.bbc.co.uk/news/world-middle-east-26841410#:~:text=Deep%20in%20the%20deserts%20of

66   al-Qurʾān 14:24-26.

67   Ṣaḥīḥ al-Bukhārī 1043.

68   Ṣaḥīḥ al-Bukhārī 2731/2732.

69   Ṣaḥīḥ Muslim 746.

70   al-Qurʾān 15:9.

71   Hamza Andreas Tzortzis. The Divine Reality: God, Islam & the Mirage of Atheism. Hong Kong: Lion Rock Publishing; 2019.

72   al-Qurʾān 17:88.

73   al-Qurʾān 11:13.

74   al-Qurʾān 2:23.

75   al-Qurʾān 10:38.

76   Jāmiʿ al-Bayān 29/156.

77   Palmer E. A study of the Qurân. Vol. 1. Sagwan Press; 1900.

78   Mishkāh al-Maṣābīḥ 3025.

79   al-Qurʾān 1:1-7.

Printed in Great Britain
by Amazon

46624315R00069